ORCHESTRAL SYMBOLISM IN WAGNER'S
DAS RHEINGOLD

BY MARTIN S. RICHTER

Originally published as "Symbolism In The Orchestration Of Wagner's <u>Das
Rheingold</u>."

COPYRIGHT © 1980, 1982, 2012 BY MARTIN S. RICHTER
PITTSBURGH, PA   USA

ISBN-13: 978-1478223481
ISBN-10: 1478223480

www.martinsrichter.com

DEDICATION

For my loving grandfather, Harry Baskin.

TABLE OF CONTENTS

INTRODUCTION i

AUTHOR'S NOTE.. v

LIST OF ABBREVIATIONS vi

NOTES ON NAMING LEITMOTIVES..................................... vii

HOW TO READ EXAMPLES vii

THE RING MOTIVE.. 1

TABLE I: RING MOTIVE SCORINGS 15

THE SMITHS MOTIVE 16

TABLE II: COMPARISON OF RING AND
    SMITHS MOTIVES 23

THE GIANTS MOTIVE... 24

TABLE III: COMPARISON OF RING, SMITHS,
    AND GIANTS MOTIVES 33

SORROW MOTIVE... 34

TABLE IV: COMPARISON OF RING, SMITHS,
    GIANTS, AND SORROW MOTIVES.............................. 46

VALHALLA MOTIVE 47

TABLE V: SCORINGS OF THE VALHALLA MOTIVE
    SHARED BY THE RING, SMITHS, GIANTS, OR
    SORROW MOTIVES 53

RENUNCIATION OF LOVE MOTIVE..................................... 54

STOPPED HORN 59

TREMOLO STRING COMBINATIONS.................................... 62

ANALYSES OF INSTRUMENTAL SECTIONS......................... 71

    ANALYSIS OF SCORINGS VS.
    SYMBOLIC MEANINGS—PRELUDE 72

TABLE VI: PRELUDE SCORINGS 73

SUMMARY OF SCORINGS USED IN PRELUDE 76

PRELUDE ANALYSIS.. 78

HORN CANON ANALYSIS: PRELUDE 79

ANALYSIS OF SCORINGS VS.
SYMBOLIC MEANINGS—FIRST INTERLUDE........................... 81

TABLE VII: FIRST INTERLUDE SCORINGS 82

SUMMARY OF SCORINGS USED IN
FIRST INTERLUDE 85

FIRST INTERLUDE ANALYSIS 87

ANALYSIS OF SCORINGS VS.
SYMBOLIC MEANINGS—
SECOND AND THIRD INTERLUDES.. 90

TABLE VIII: SECOND INTERLUDE SCORINGS........................... 92

TABLE IX: THIRD INTERLUDE SCORINGS 98

SUMMARY OF SCORINGS USED IN
SECOND AND THIRD INTERLUDES..103

SECOND AND THIRD INTERLUDE ANALYSES.........................109

ANALYSIS OF TWO VOCAL EXCERPTS..113

ANALYSIS OF LOGE'S NARRATIVE 113

ANALYSIS OF SCENE THREE EXCERPT 119

SCORINGS OF MOTIVIC STATEMENTS
AND THEIR SYMBOLS..122

TABLE X: ORCHESTRAL SYMBOLS 123

SUMMARY...125

INTRODUCTION

As he created <u>Der Ring des Nibelungen,</u> Richard Wagner envisioned a compositional cosmos greater than any entity known during his time. His concept of *Gesamtkunstwerk*, an all-embracing artform, sought to integrate words, music, drama, and movement into a unified structure. He wanted all the pieces of this structure to reinforce each other on a variety of levels, thereby creating a web of meaning that would provide total immersion in the self-contained virtual world of the <u>Ring</u>.

Wagner developed numerous devices to achieve the <u>Ring's</u> compositional unity and unique identity. He commissioned new instruments, utilized alliteration in the dialogue, and even designed a new theater to house the "artwork of the future." Most notably, Wagner used his expanded orchestra as more than an accompanist to the singers on stage. It is a quasi-character, a commentator on the drama. In the <u>Ring</u>, the orchestra becomes an integral part of the dramatic action. At times, it is used as a sole force for furthering the plot.

Wagner accomplished this feat through his innovative and systematic use of leitmotives. These recurring themes represent characters or ideas. Throughout the music dramas, the leitmotives transmogrify and evolve to match the progression of fluid ideas in the story. They accumulate to form a supplementary, "encoded" level of meaning that augments the power of Wagner's music to fuse with his dramatic action, and allows him to comment on the thoughts and actions of the characters.

Motives often vary in orchestration as they reappear. A motive may first appear in the violins, and later be found in the winds. In <u>Das Rheingold</u>, the specific scorings recur and accumulate in a systematic fashion that allows for direct symbolic association between instrumentation and dramatic intent akin to the evolution of the motives themselves.

Wagner's choice of instruments to score the leitmotives reveals another heretofore uncharted layer of encoded meaning embedded in the fabric of the music drama. When scored for horn, a leitmotive associated with the ring itself might indicate the ring as the prize of the gods. The same theme changes its character when it is played by a clarinet-bassoon combination. The foggy, gloomy sound of these instruments signifies Alberich's connection with the ring. The result is a connotative symbolic level to the leitmotive—its shade of meaning changes consistently with each different scoring.

An examination of this orchestral symbolism layer allows us to understand Das Rheingold on a whole new level. Audiences can follow the choice of instrumentation to grasp new dramatic associations, and directors may choose to emphasize different elements of the production to reinforce the intent of the music. A conductor might find new insights in the interpretation of the score, and opt to highlight the role of certain instruments accordingly. The dramatic nature of the instrumentation could serve as another aid in unifying the structure of the music, as well as enhancing Wagner's dramatic and philosophical intent in portraying a given subject.

An assertion of Wagner's intentional and systematic use of scoring to create a new layer of specific meaning into the Ring requires considerable evidence to substantiate the claim. Wagner himself offers a few hints in this direction. In 1852,[1] he describes the "…speaking-faculty of the Orchestra … of uttering the unspeakable… which the Orchestra can express with greatest definition, and indeed, in union …with Gesture… That which Poetry could not speak out… is imparted to the ear by … the Orchestra." In the same section, he tells us that the orchestra has "the capability of awaking forebodings and remembrances."

Scholars generally agree that the preceding refers to leitmotives and their power to supplement and reinforce other elements of the drama through the language of instrumental music and its "heightened power of speech."

---

[1] Richard Wagner, Opera and Drama, trans. William Ashton Ellis, from Richard Wagner's Prose Works, Vol. 2. (London: Kegan Paul, Trench, Trübner & Co., Ltd., 1900), 316-336.

Wagner appears to indicate a step beyond leitmotives, into the realm of orchestral timbre, when he says that extra-musical ideas are shown "...plainly enough by the Instruments of the orchestra themselves, whereof each for itself... speaks out quite clearly and intelligibly." In the same passage, Wagner also mentions "tone-figures peculiar to the individual character of specially appropriate instruments, and shaping themselves into the specific Orchestral-melody" to fuse gesture and instrumental music. Later, he asserts that, in order to elevate instrumental music to the point of synthesis, a composer must discover "...the most varied orchestral idioms... so long as the message of the Orchestra is too monochrome to answer these motives' individuality, ... it prove[s] a disturbing factor, because not yet completely satisfying..."[2] From the preceding, it would seem that Wagner views insufficiently varied orchestration as a cause of incomplete artistic expression. He intends his choice of instrumentation as a means to perfect the fusion between instrumental music, poetry, and gesture. Indeed, a year earlier, Wagner describes a "...more symbolic treatment of the instrumental orchestra..."[3] to augment the power of his musical expression. Taking this into account, it is not too great a leap to suppose that Wagner also intended his scoring choices to add an extra layer of meaning to his leitmotives.

To prove this, I will focus on the first of the four music dramas in the Ring, Das Rheingold. Here, Wagner introduces us to his self-contained world, and works hardest to establish entities and contexts. The result is a deliberate, almost pedantic display of themes and dramatic characterization. Such a literal presentation offers the audience a solid aesthetic foundation in Wagner's virtual world. It establishes basic concepts, and prepares the audience for the evolution of musical and dramatic ideas as they blend and change throughout the course of the Ring cycle. The scoring of Das Rheingold is similarly methodical. Dramatic association with various instruments is at its most direct in this first of the four music dramas. It will become more general in the other three as all elements of the music dramas intermingle and grow more fluid.

---

2 Wagner, 370.
3 Richard Wagner, A Communication To My Friends, trans. William Ashton Ellis, from Richard Wagner's Prose Works, Vol. 1. (London: Kegan Paul, Trench, Trübner & Co., Ltd., 1892), 374.

I will provide evidence of orchestral symbolism by tracing frequently recurring motives throughout <u>Das Rheingold</u> in relation to their literal/dramatic contexts, and by citing examples of specific scorings that correlate with particular shades of meaning as they reappear throughout the work. These subtexts will not be limited to individual motivic statements. Rather, the scorings will retain their extra-musical associations across several leitmotives.. The connotative links will become evident by means of the similarity of scoring and accumulation. Using this method, we can discover a symbolic commonality that mirrors the scoring choices. In addition, I will discuss sections of the work where the orchestration plays a key role, and discuss its implication on performance practice. I hope that revealing this layer of meaning may further aid the reader in understanding the multi-leveled concept of *Gesamtkunstwerk*, in which every aspect of the music drama is an equally important member in forming its whole.

Even a century before the advent of computer simulation games, Wagner anticipated the level of encoding and detail necessary to formulate a complete virtual world, one that allows the audience to immerse itself thoroughly. He controlled the words, the visual images, and especially, the music. The result is an environment in which every stimulus, including the orchestration, allows us to discover new significance in the universe of the <u>Ring</u>.

AUTHOR'S NOTE

I first encountered <u>Das Rheingold</u> in the 1970's as an undergraduate at Carnegie-Mellon. I had just broken my wrist, which forced me to stop playing music, but also allowed me to learn how to really listen. It was a strange piece of music to my ears, with none of the conventions I'd expected in an opera. The leitmotives seemed to hold the piece together, but I sensed that there was another unifying element. I was determined to make sense of it, so I played my Solti LPs over and over.

After several listenings, I began to notice the patchwork-style of orchestration. The colors seemed to change every few bars, in an almost kaleidoscopic fashion. Following a hunch, I began to compare statements of leitmotives. Many seemed to recur with identical scorings. Could this repetition be another element of musical form? Then, I compared the dramatic contexts that accompanied these similar statements. They held common elements as well. Patterns began to form—the scorings shaded the leitmotives in very predictable ways. Wagner's choice of instruments paralleled the drama! The orchestral shading revealed a layer of subtext beyond leitmotives. I gathered supporting evidence from the orchestral score, and from Wagner's own writings. The result of this evidence, and my conclusions, is this book.

Thirty-two years after its first printing, I have revised the original text, and added new sections of analysis. Perceiving <u>Das Rheingold</u> on this level enabled me to understand it in much greater depth. I hope my findings can lead others toward a deeper appreciation of <u>Das Rheingold</u>, and inspire conductors, performers, and stage directors to utilize the symbols hidden in Wagner's orchestration to achieve their own optimal performances.

I would like to express my appreciation to the following for their help in the production of this study.

Dr. J. L. Hunt   Mr. L. Geissel,
Mr. W. J. Cadman III   Mr. C. Madge
Mr. R. Fellner,

......and of course, my family.

LIST OF ABBREVIATIONS

Vn .... Violin	Tr .... Trumpet
Br .... Viola	BTr .... Bass Trumpet
Vc .... Cello	Pos .... Trombone
Cb .... Double Bass	CBP .... Contrabass Trombone
Pauk .... Tympani	TTb .... Tenor Tuba
Cym .... Cymbal	BTb ..... Bass Tuba
Anv ... Anvil	CBT .... Contrabass Tuba
KlF .... Piccolo	/ .... Two instruments playing one after another
Fl .... Flute	( ) .... Complement or underscoring
Hb .... Oboe	Trem .... Tremolo
Eng. Hn .... English Horn	Hn .... Horn
Cl .... Clarinet	St Hn .... Stopped Horn
BCl .... Bass Clarinet	Vce .... Voice
Fag .... Bassoon	

NOTE ON NAMING LEITMOTIVES

Labels for leitmotives are approximations that have varied according to their historical contexts and translations. For purposes of identification, I will use names that have been generally accepted.

HOW TO READ EXAMPLES

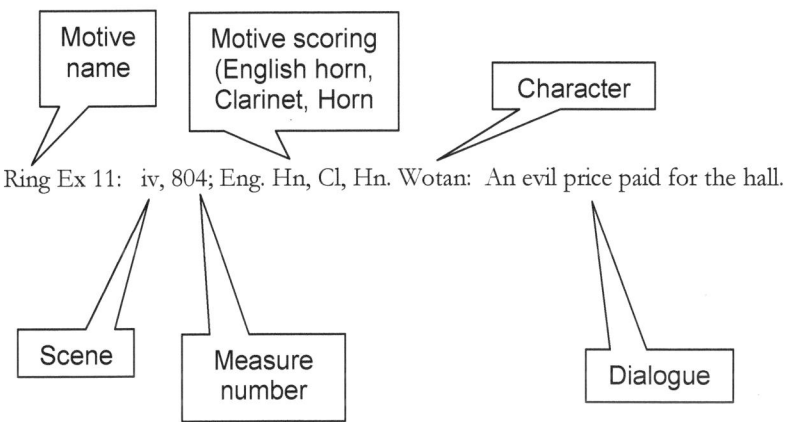

Motive name

Motive scoring (English horn, Clarinet, Horn

Character

Ring Ex 11: iv, 804; Eng. Hn, Cl, Hn. Wotan: An evil price paid for the hall.

Scene

Measure number

Dialogue

ORCHESTRAL SYMBOLISM IN
WAGNER'S <u>DAS RHEINGOLD</u>

The most frequently recurring motives in <u>Das Rheingold</u> provide the most evidence to show how changing orchestration of a leitmotive changes its meaning. Note that these motives all touch on different aspects of the drama, so they constitute the most complete presentation of examples. We will examine the Ring, Nibelung Smiths, Giants, Sorrow, Valhalla, and Renunciation of Love motives.

The Ring motive

The Ring motive, which appears over 60 times in <u>Das Rheingold,</u> portrays the ring itself as passive in nature. Although the ring is cursed, it is neither inherently good nor evil, but assumes the qualities of those with whom it comes into contact. Because every character uses the ring differently, the ring's quality is similarly multifaceted. Wagner scores the Ring motive in many different ways to reflect this.

Wagner uses the combination of horn and bassoon five times, three times alone and twice with strings. Each of these statements makes a reference to the ring as payment. In the following three instances, when the Ring motive is played by the horn and bassoon alone, the payment refers to the ransom of gold requested of the gods by the giants.

Ring Ex 1: iv, 574; Hn, Fag. Fafner: Now add the final part of the ransom.

Ring Ex 2: iv, 756; Hn, Fag. Fafner: Now blink upon Freia's face. You'll see the ring no more.

Ring Ex 3: iv, 803; Hn, Fag. Wotan: An evil price paid for the hall.

In Example 1, the giants are trying to collect the remainder of their ransom of gold from the gods. All that remains to be forfeited, say the giants, is the ring on Wotan's finger. Wotan insists on his right to keep the ring. At this point, the Ring motive appears in the horn and bassoon as Fafner orders Wotan to add the ring to the pile of gold. The second example of horn and bassoon appears when the giants look for a way to divide the hoard. Loge advises Fafner to take the treasure, and Fasolt to take the ring. The giants argue about this judgment, and Fafner slays Fasolt. Fafner then wrests the ring from the corpse, and tells the gods that the ransom has been paid as the horn and bassoon play the Ring motive. The third example occurs when Wotan wishes to descend to Erda to learn of his future. Fricka suggests that he remain instead at Valhalla. The Ring motive then appears to accompany Wotan's gloomy reflection on the price that he paid for his castle.

In the following example, the horn and bassoon play the Ring motive in combination with the strings. Tremolo violin, viola, and cello are added to represent Fafner's mental instability as he grabs for the ring, which he believes is the payment owed him.[4]

Ring Ex 4: iv, 747; Hn, Fag, Trem. Vn, Br, Vc.   Fafner: The ring is mine!

There is also a combination that includes a cello with the horn-bassoon scoring.

Ring Ex 5:   i, 566;.   Hn, Fag, Vc   Alberich: I wrest from the rock the
                                          gold, forging the ring of revenge.

This example occurs toward the end of the first scene, where Alberich, after attempting to court the Rheinmaidens, decides to compensate for his rejection by stealing their gold as his "payment."

---

[4] Wagner often uses string tremolo to add a surreal dimension to certain moments. At times, the device is used to represent mental instability. (See article on tremolo.)

While the horn-bassoon scoring of the Ring motive refers to the ring as payment, Wagner scores the Ring motive in the horns alone to refer to the ring's connection with the gods of Valhalla on three separate occasions.

Ring Ex 6:   Int. 1, 48;   Hn.   (Discussed in Int. 1 analysis.)

Ring Ex 7:   ii, 74;   Hn.   Wotan: Did Fricka harbor such greed
                                        when she craved for the hall?

Ring Ex 8:   ii, 679;   Hn.   Fricka: Would the golden trinket make
                                        some jewelry?

All three examples refer to the gods of Valhalla, most notably Fricka. In the interlude example, Wagner lays the groundwork for future horn references by placing the motive directly before the overture to the second scene as Wotan and Fricka lie asleep in a flowery bank.[5] The second example occurs when Wotan reminds Fricka of the glory of the hall. The setting appears again when Fricka asks Loge about why the gods want the Rheingold. Since the horn is generally connected with other godly references in <u>Das</u> Rheingold[6], it seems that Wagner used the horn to establish a reference to the gods of Valhalla that a listener might identify as an underlying unifying quality in the work.

In the following examples using English horn and clarinet, the common element seems to be the ring as guarantor of world rule. Note that the horn is added in the first three examples, and the bassoon is added in the following four examples. The examples that use a horn refer to Wotan as world ruler.

Ring Ex 9:   ii, 1008;   Eng. Hn, Cl, Hn.   Wotan: Our youth that left us
                                                    returns when I ravish the gold.

Ring Ex 10:   iv, 247;   Eng. Hn, Cl, Hn.   Wotan puts on the ring.

Ring Ex 11:   iv, 804;   Eng. Hn, Cl, Hn.   Wotan: An evil price paid for
                                                    the hall.

---

[5] This overture is made up of the first statements of the Valhalla motive, which is scored for full brass with tubas used in place of horns. This will be discussed further in the article concerning the Valhalla motive.
[6] Notably, the strongest statement of the Golden Apples motive (ii, 323) appears in the horn accompanying the voice.

Example 9 occurs near the end of the second scene when the gods seem about to perish from lack of the youth-giving golden apples. Wotan, even though weakened, takes stock of himself and draws on his power of command to launch a campaign to win back his power. The statement of the Ring motive at this point echoes Wotan's aspirations to rule the world. The second example refers to Wotan's role as world ruler in that the act of wearing the ring grants him infinite power. Example 11 occurs one bar after Example 3 (Hn, Fag) in which Wotan reflects on the price of his power.

In the examples that use the bassoon, Alberich is named as world ruler.

Ring Ex 12:	i, 534;	Eng. Hn, Cl, Fag.	Alberich: So earth's kingdom is mine to possess through you?
Ring Ex 13:	ii, 604;	Eng. Hn, Cl, Fag.	Loge: He (Alberich) thinks it now the worthiest good.
Ring Ex 14:	ii, 669;	Eng. Hn, Cl, Fag.	Loge: ...and grant its owner the world.
Ring Ex 15:	ii, 713;	Eng. Hn, Cl, Fag.	Loge: A rune of magic makes the gold a ring. No one knows it.

The first example in this group occurs near the end of the first scene where Alberich, his eyes fixed on the gold, exclaims in wonderment that he can now satisfy his craving for absolute power. Example 13 occurs when Loge explains how Alberich came to power. He says that Alberich now values the stolen gold above all else. The third example in this group occurs shortly after Loge's explanation that possession of the ring grants its owner (Alberich) world rule. In Example 15, Loge explains the power of the gold after Fafner asks him why Alberich wants it so badly. Wagner amplifies this scoring in the second scene which pictures Wotan plotting to wrest control of the ring from Alberich.[7] In a sense, Wotan is "trying out" Alberich's scoring as he envisions himself in Alberich's present role as world ruler.

---

[7] This scoring is possibly related to the clarinet-bassoon combination mentioned later.

The addition of tremolo strings emphasizes the dreamlike fantasy of this moment.[8]

| Ring Ex 16: | ii, 704; | Hb, Eng. Hn/Cl, Fag, Trem. Vn, Br, Vc. | Wotan: Control of the circlet might be wise, to my thinking. |

Wagner uses the cello four times in his scoring of the Ring Motive. Throughout the opera, cello scoring of various motives often refers to thoughts of hiding, secrecy, and isolation. Each of these cello examples combines the ring's reference to riches with a reference to hiding and privacy.

Ring Ex 17:	ii, 3;	Vc.	Fricka: Wotan, my lord, awaken! Wotan (still asleep): My hall of blessed delights…
Ring Ex 18:	ii, 71;	Vc.	Fricka: … once you men lust for might.
Ring Ex 19:	ii, 674;	Vc.	Wotan: Runes of riches hide in its (gold's) ruddy gleam.
Ring Ex 20:	iv, 167;	Vc.	Wotan: You really call it your own?

The first example in this group occurs at the beginning of the second scene as Wotan lies asleep on a flowery bank. His thoughts of riches are submerged in dreams and thus are hidden from the real world. In Example 18, Fricka reprimands Wotan for dealing deceitfully in order to gain riches. The cello scoring recalls the mood of private personal glory found earlier in Example 17. In Example 19, the cello alternates with the trombone, asking us to consider the double-edged sword of the ring's hidden riches versus its hidden curse.[9] The last example is taken from near the beginning of the fourth scene where Wotan demands that Alberich forfeit the ring. When Alberich complains about the gods stealing his ring, Wotan asks incredulously if Alberich is, in fact, the rightful owner of the treasure. He then accuses Alberich of hiding the truth from him.

---

[8] See the article on string tremolo.
[9] See discussion of the Ring motive in the trombone.

Wagner also uses the cello toward the end of the opera as Wotan reflects upon the glory of his palace.

Ring Ex 21:   iv, 903;   Vc, Hn/Cl.   Wotan: From morning to evening...I
                                            worked for its winning.

Although he is onstage with the other gods, Wotan is quite isolated from them in his thoughts. His "soliloquy" carries his own personal reflection on his struggle to win the palace. As Wotan ponders this struggle, the Ring motive is played in the cello, combined with the horn first, then the clarinet. The symbolic intent behind this particular scoring is possibly a presentation of the two sides who took part in the struggle: Valhalla (horn) and the Nibelungs (clarinet).[10] The cello scoring remains constant to preserve Wotan's aura of intimacy in this private, though seemingly public speech. One could identify this particular example as a very deliberate scoring choice because prior to their entrances in this statement of the Ring motive, the horn has been tacit for six bars, the cello for twenty five bars, and the clarinet has not played for thirty five bars.

The trombone plays the Ring motive twice by itself, both times referring to the curse of the ring.

Ring Ex 22:   iv, 279;   Pos.   Alberich: Let none rejoice owning the ring.

Ring Ex 23:   iv, 782;   Pos.   Loge: Your foes murder their friends for the
                                   gold.
                                   Wotan: What a horror enchains me!

The Curse motive is always scored for trombone, suggesting that the instrument has some symbolic meaning in that direction.

Wagner uses the combination of viola and cello three separate times.

Ring Ex 24:   ii, 4;   Br, Vc.   Wotan (still asleep): My hall of blessed
                                      delights, guarded at door and gate.

---

[10] Wagner regularly uses the clarinet to refer to the Nibelungs. See discussion of the Ring motive in the clarinet-bass clarinet-bassoon.

Ring Ex 25:   ii, 803;   Br, Vc.   Fafner: Let your Freia remain here. Smaller payment now will suit us.

Ring Ex 26:   iv, 45;   Br, Vc.   Alberich: Thievish… gang; (aside) I may give them the gold, as I have the ring!

In all three cases, the dominant element is the aspect of the ring which inspires characters to covet material possessions. In Example 24, a cello statement of the Ring motive begins when Wotan dreams of his hall (see Ex 17), and the viola and cello play the Ring motive together when Wotan dreams of the guards that hold his fortress secure. In Example 25, Fafner turns down a reward of female companionship for one of gold. Material wealth means more to him than a wife. The ring as prize to be coveted also appears in Example 26. Alberich willingly gives the gods his gold as he concentrates his thoughts on the ring that serves as a tool for obtaining supreme material riches. The combination of viola and cello is also used in connection with Loge in the more indirect reference to evil desire as part of his general character.[11]

An odd combination of instruments that appears only twice is clarinet, English horn, trumpet, and bass trumpet. It occurs at two spots where Alberich kisses his ring.[12] Since this combination is used so sparingly in the opera, it is difficult to discern Wagner's specific symbolic meaning. Perhaps it is somehow related to the notion of Alberich as world ruler as expressed in the English horn, clarinet, bassoon combination discussed earlier.

The combination of clarinet and bassoon occurs seven times in Wagner's scoring of the Ring motive.

Ring Ex 27:   i, 512;   Cl, Fag.   Rheinmaidens: Loveliest Alberich! Can't you laugh too?

---

[11] Of the 45 statements of Loge's motive that appear in <u>Das Rheingold</u>, 19 are scored for viola and cello, including the statements that introduce the motive. When we consider only those statements that accompany vocal text, the ratio is close to 1:2. As a result, this scoring combination becomes Loge's "signature" timbre.
[12] iii, 389 and iv, 61. The bass trumpet first appears prominently when sunlight illuminates the gold in scene one. Alberich may be remembering the origin of his prize.

Ring Ex 28:	ii, 756;	Cl, Fag.	Loge: The Nibelung is skilled in wicked aims.
Ring Ex 29:	ii, 808;	Cl, Fag.	Fafner: The Nibelung's ruddy gold...
Ring Ex 30:	ii, 663;	Cl, Fag.	Loge: Yet, when it is fashioned into a circlet, it will grant highest power . . .
Ring Ex 31:	iii, 307;	Cl, Fag.	Loge: Admit, it's not an easy job (to retrieve the gold from Nibelheim.)
Ring Ex 32:	iv, 139;	Cl, Fag.	Alberich: He who forged me the first (Tarnhelm), let him repeat it.
Ring Ex 33:	iv, 743;	Cl, Fag.	Fasolt throws himself on Fafner.

Most of these examples refer to the Nibelungs directly. Three examples require clarification. In Example 30, Loge's accompaniment describes the Nibelungs as the ones who have fashioned the gold into a ring. In relating this scoring combination to the English horn-clarinet-bassoon combination discussed earlier, it is interesting to note the proximity of Example 30 to Example 14 where Wagner notes the identity of the one who first fashions the ring, then he refers to the idea of Nibelung rule. In Example 31, Loge and Wotan discuss the job of retrieving the gold from Nibelheim, directing the statement as a reference to Alberich. Example 33 is an indirect reference to the treachery of the Nibelungs as Fasolt and Fafner now lower themselves to the same brother-against-brother rivalry that Alberich and Mime expressed earlier in the opera.

The following are examples of scorings of the Ring motive that are related to the clarinet-bassoon combination.

Ring Ex 34:	i, 532;	Hb, Cl, Fag.	Alberich listens to the sisters' chatter.
Ring Ex 35:	i, 544;	Hb, Cl, Fag, Fl.	Rheinmaidens: For love has made him insane! Ha Ha Ha!
Ring Ex 36:	iii, 302;	Hb, Cl, Fag, Fl, Trem Br.	Mime: . . . and such is the thanks that fool has won. (referring to his beating by Alberich)

| Ring Ex 37: | iv, 577; | Hn, Cl, Fag. | Wotan: Ask as much as you will, but all the world cannot make me give up the ring. |

The first three examples add an oboe, possibly to represent innocence.[13] Example 35 is taken from the same passage as Example 34, and refers directly to Alberich. In Example 36, the tremolo viola is added, possibly to refer to the insanity that caused Alberich to beat his brother (See article on tremolo). In Example 37, Wotan lowers himself to the level of the Nibelung in his obsessive desire to keep the ring. Note the use of the horn to represent Valhalla in combination with the clarinet-bassoon reference to the Nibelung.

A combination related to the clarinet-bassoon combination is clarinet-bass clarinet-bassoon. This scoring seems to be a reference to the hate connected with the ring. Note that Example 38, the first statement of this combination, shows the Nibelung expressing his hate. Likewise, the Nibelung scorn motive is typically stated in the clarinet.

Ring Ex 38:	iv, 394;	Cl, BCl, Fag.	Alberich: Let its owner never be blessed.
Ring Ex 39:	iv, 735;	Cl, BCl, Fag.	Fafner: When in desire to woo (Freia), you thought not to share.
Ring Ex 40:	iv, 745;	Cl, BCl, Fag, (Eng. Hn).	Fasolt: Away, you cheater, mine is the ring; I bought it for Freia's glance!

In Example 39, the giants discuss how to divide up the ransom, and this discussion becomes a quarrel in which Fafner grows hateful of Fasolt and accuses him of sharing Freia unfairly in the past. In Example 40, Wagner adds the English horn when Fasolt says that he bought the ring for Freia's glance. Perhaps this is related to the English horn-clarinet combinations discussed earlier as world rule through possession of the ring now goes to the giants.

---

[13] In The Forging of the Ring, (Cambridge University Press, 1976), Curt von Westernhagen asserts that Wagner called the oboe "the naive-tragic instrument." (p. 52) Oboe statements of Freia's motive tend to refer to Freia's beauty and peril. Violin scorings generally refer to tender feelings or helplessness.

Wagner uses the combination of violin and viola to present warnings to the gods. There are five separate examples of this scoring.

Ring Ex 41:	iii, 219;	Vn, Br. (Cl, Fag)	Mime: . . . and forge into shapes.
Ring Ex 42:	iii, 517;	Vn, Br. (Fl, Hb, Hn, Cl, Fag).	Alberich: The gold will win me control of the planet!
Ring Ex 43:	Int. 3, 8	Vn, Br.	discussed in Int. 3 analysis.
Ring Ex 44:	iv, 137;	Vn, Br. (Cl, Fag).	Alberich: Accursed thief! But wait awhile…
Ring Ex 45:	iv, 647;	Vn, Br (Pos, Fl, Hb, Eng. Hn, Cl, Fag).	Erda: A dark day dawns for the gods.

In the first example, Mime tells Wotan and Loge of the terrible power of their enemy, Alberich. In Examples 42 and 44, Alberich warns the gods of his plans to take control through the ring's power. Note that in all these examples, the warnings deal with the Nibelungs' attempt to wrest control of the earth from the gods. This reference is further strengthened by the presence of clarinet-bassoon combinations, either accompanying the motive, or nearby, most notably in Example 44 where a clarinet-bassoon scoring of the Ring motive immediately follows the violin-viola combination.

Another form of a warning to the gods appears twice in the combination of horn, bass clarinet, and bassoon. This scoring differs in meaning from the violin-viola examples in that it expresses a threat, rather than a warning, to Wotan. This scoring combines the horn reference to the gods, with the clarinet-bass clarinet-bassoon reference to hate.

Ring Ex 46:	ii, 842;	Hn, BCl, Fag.	Fafner: . . . unless you give in ransom, the Rheingold fair and red . . .
Ring Ex 47:	iv, 211;	Hn, BCl, Fag.	Alberich: Guard yourself, conquering god!

In Example 46, the giants threaten to keep Freia unless the gods give them the Rheingold. In Example 47, Alberich threatens Wotan with the Nibelungs' curse, should Wotan obtain the ring.

When the viola section alone carries the Ring motive, Wagner expresses a feeling of denial of either love or power in connection with the ring.

Ring Ex 48:	i, 492;	Br.	Wellgunde: . . .we are safe and need not care, for love rules all that's living. Nothing that loves flees affection.
Ring Ex 49:	Int. 1, 44;	Br.	Discussed under Int. 1 analysis.
Ring Ex 50:	ii, 757;	Br.	Loge: What you do has to be clever, if you would overcome the thief.
Ring Ex 51:	iii, 670;	Br.	Loge: Your ring makes you brave.
Ring Ex 52:	iv, 648;	Br.	Erda: I warn you, give up the ring.

In the first example, the Rheinmaidens discuss whether they need to fear that Alberich's will steal the gold. When they come to the conclusion that he is love-starved, and poses no threat of forging the ring, they decide to deny him their love. Example 50 immediately follows a clarinet-bassoon scoring of the Ring motive, and helps complete the orchestral illustration of denying the Nibelung the power of the Ring. In Example 51, the viola scoring emphasizes Loge's next line to the Nibelung (paraphrased): But what if it were stolen? In Example 52, Erda urges Wotan to deny himself the Ring. A related scoring of bassoon-viola appears twice near the end of the first scene. These examples suggest the love denied the Nibelung.

Ring Ex 53:	i, 502;	Fag, Br.	Flosshilde: I fear him not (Alberich)... I was nearly scorched, he was so hot.
Ring Ex 54:	i, 536;	Fag, Br.	Alberich: If, love be denied me, my cunning shall win me delight.

In Example 53, Flosshilde sees that she has no need to fear denying Alberich her love. In Example 54, Alberich refers directly to the love denied him.

The combination of oboe, bassoon and horn appears twice (once with clarinet) in the third scene.

Ring Ex 55:	iii, 267;	Cl, Hb, Fag, Hn.	Mime: …I as freeman should command.
Ring Ex 56:	iii, 380;	Hb, Fag, Hn.	Alberich: … that I lurk and watch, unseen by all.

Both times it signifies the Nibelungs' aspirations to absolute power. This is not a strong reference, as the motive appears only once in each form.

Bassoon examples appear three times in the opera.

Ring Ex 57:	Int. 1, 40	Fag/Hn.	discussed in Int. 1 analysis.
Ring Ex 58:	ii, 921;	Fag/Hn.	Froh: My heart has stopped. Loge: I have it; Learn what you're lacking!
Ring Ex 59:	iv, 192;	Hn/Fag.	Alberich: You would have gladly stolen the gold yourself, had it been as easy to forge as to steal.

Since they appear in close proximity with horn scorings, these are referred to as bassoon/horn scorings. These differ from horn-bassoon combinations in that the two do not play together, but alternate. Since the horn is used to refer to Valhalla and fairness, and the bassoon refers to Nibelheim and gloom, the scoring shows the gods sinking to the level of the Nibelungs, or vice versa, depending on the order of the horn and bassoon statements. In Example 58, Froh speaks of the mist that weakens him. This is followed by Loge's suggestion of hope. The change in scoring from bassoon to horn shows the transition from gloom to light as Loge attempts to raise the gods' spirits. In Example 59, the bassoon follows the horn as Alberich accuses the gods of stooping to evil intent.

The following combinations play the Ring motive only once, but we can still draw some conclusions about their relationship to scorings previously discussed.

There exist two double reed scorings in which characters mention the idea of world rule.

Ring Ex 60:	i, 467;	Hb, Fag, Eng. Hn, (Fl).	Wellgunde: … and world rule is the prize …
Ring Ex 61:	ii, 665;	Hb, Fag.	Loge: … it will give highest power

These two examples would seem to bear a resemblance to either the English horn-clarinet-bassoon scoring (Nibelung rule), or the oboe-bassoon-horn (Nibelung aspiration to power) scoring found in Examples 55 and 56, since they both refer to the power of the ring. Example 60 represents the first time we hear the ring motive. The vocal line cements the association between the double reed voicing, the motive, and the power inherent in the ring.

A horn-clarinet combination appears once at the end of the second scene. This is the point where, after being reprimanded by Fricka, Wotan decides to go to Nibelheim to recover the Rheingold. The horn symbolizes the gods, and the clarinet seems to be a reference to Nibelheim.

As mentioned earlier, the oboe represents a mood of naïveté and tragedy. Here are two unrelated scorings which use the oboe in combination with single reed instruments.

Ring Ex 62:	ii, 575;	Cl, Hb.	Loge: I asked all that lives and loves, but was met with laughs.
Ring Ex 63:	iv, 791;	Hb, Fl, Trem. Vn, Br.	Wotan: I must descend to Erda.

The first example is discussed in the analysis of Loge's narrative. In example 63, Wagner blends the sorrow of Wotan, desperate for knowledge, with the surreal effect of the string tremolo.

One example that employs a stopped horn.[14]

---

[14] See article on stopped horn.

| Ring Ex 64: | iv, 236; | St. Hn, Hb, Eng. Hn, (Cl). | Alberich: Ha! Defeated! Destroyed! |

The stopped horn is used to represent an insult or scorn, in this context, the insult of Alberich's defeat as delivered by Wotan. The combination is perhaps related to the English horn-clarinet-horn scoring (world rule), in that the moment marks a victory for Wotan.

Two miscellaneous string scorings occur, neither of which have any clear symbolic meaning.

| Ring Ex 65: | iii, 508; | Vc, Cb. | Alberich: Watch the wonder I'm planning. |

| Ring Ex 66: | Int. 2, 87 | Vn, Br, Vc. | discussed in Int. 2 analysis. |

The first example might be construed as a reference to the secrecy and darkness associated with other cello-double bass scorings, as Alberich dreams of his secret plan. Example 66 is an interlude statement, so we cannot tie it directly to dramatic action.

The variety of Ring motive scorings reflects the many shades of meaning inherent in the notion of the ring. The connotative meanings make us aware of its complexity as it parallels the natures of the many stakeholders in the drama.

After examining the scorings of the Ring motive, we can form a data table comparing the instruments used in Wagner's scoring with their symbolic meaning. The correlation between a horn setting of the Ring motive, for example, and a horn setting of any other motive may not be related as directly as two similar horn settings of the same motive, but as we examine other frequently occurring motives, we will find that they share a more general contextual similarity.

TABLE I: RING MOTIVE SCORINGS

Instruments	Number of Scorings	Symbolic Meaning
Horn-Bassoon	5	Payment
Horn	3	Gods of Valhalla, Fairness, Light
English Horn-Clarinet-Horn	3	World rule for Wotan
(Oboe) English Horn-Clarinet-Bassoon	5	World rule for Alberich
Cello	5	Isolation, Privacy, Hiding
Trombone	2	Curse
Viola-Cello	3	Coveting
English Horn-Clarinet-Trumpet-Bass Trumpet	2	Alberich kisses his ring
Clarinet-Bassoon	11	Nibelungs
Clarinet-Bass Clarinet-Bassoon	3	Hate
Violin-Viola	5	Warning
Viola	5	Denial
Horn-Bass Clarinet-Bassoon	2	Threat
Oboe-Bassoon-Horn	2	Nibelung's aspiration to power
Horn/Bassoon	3	Alternation between Valhalla and Nibelheim; light and gloom
Bassoon-Viola	2	Love denied the Nibelung
Miscellaneous	7	Indeterminate

Of the 68 statements of the Ring motive found in Das Rheingold, eleven appear scored for clarinet and bassoon. This scoring refers to the Nibelungs directly. It is perhaps the most frequently used scoring of the Ring motive because the Nibelungs possess the ring for most of Das Rheingold.

Nibelung Smiths motive

The Nibelung smiths motive is one of the most memorable rhythmic figures in <u>Das Rheingold.</u> The rhythm is an onomatopoetic reference to the smiths at work in Nibelheim. It lends realism to Interludes 2 and 3, when the motive is played by eighteen anvils.[15] The smiths are the pawns of Alberich. They are completely in his thrall. Consequently, the scorings of the motivic statements reflect the various aspects of the smiths' servitude: helplessness, pain, and isolation.

As he does with the Ring motive, Wagner scores the Nibelung smiths motive in the combination of violin and viola to express a warning. This warning, however, now assumes the form of a dare. The combination is used five times in <u>Das Rheingold.</u>

Smith Ex 1:	iii, 118;	Vn, Br.	Instrumental example. Discussed in Int. 2 analysis.
Smith Ex 2:	iii, 322;	Vn, Br.	Mime crouches as Alberich enters. Mime: Keep a sharp watch! Alberich comes!
Smith Ex 3:	iii, 335;	Vn, Br.	Wotan: We'll wait your lord here.
Smith Ex 4:	iii, 750;	Vn, Br.	Alberich: Your cunning, fool, has filled you to bursting!
Smith Ex 5:	iv, 550;	Vn, Br.	Fafner: Hey, I warn you to stop up this cranny!

In Example 2, Mime warns the gods to beware Alberich, who approaches defiantly, almost in response to Wotan's call in Example 3. In example 4,

---

[15] The following anvil examples will be discussed in the analysis of Interludes 2 and 3:

Int. 2, 59 Anv, Hn, Vn, Br, Vc.; Int. 2, 67 Anv.; Int. 2, 75 Anv, Vn, Br.; Int. 3, 31 Anv.

Loge dares Alberich to prove the power of the Tarnhelm. As Alberich responds to the dare, the violin and viola play the Nibelung smiths motive. In Example 5, Fafner makes a plainer reference to a warning when he tells Loge how to stack the gold.

Wagner scores the Ring motive for horn to connect it with the gods of Valhalla. When Wagner scores the Nibelung smiths motive in the horn, he points out two qualities strongly associated with the gods (especially Fricka): fairness and justice.

Smith Ex 6:	iii, 185;	Hn.	Mime: Once, in our carefree smithing days, we made gear for our women.
Smith Ex 7:	iii, 657;	Hn.	Loge: Let me warn you not to make enemies ...
Smith Ex 8:	iv, 482;	Hn.	Fafner scrutinizes the horde.
Smith Ex 9:	iv, 499;	Hn.	Fafner: Still more this way!
Smith Ex 10:	iv, 727;	Hn.	Fasolt: Halt, greedy one! Give me some (gold) too.

Example 6 shows the most direct reference to the gods, as it indirectly refers to the horn scoring of the Ring motive in which Fricka asks Loge about forging the gold into jewelry (Ring motive, Ex. 8). In Example 7, Loge warns Alberich to rule with a just hand. Fafner tries to judge his golden ransom fairly in Examples 8 and 9. Example 10 shows Fasolt telling Fafner to be fair when dividing the gold.

Cello scorings of the Ring motive allow the cello to portray of the deep isolation within the ring. When Wagner scores the Nibelung smiths motive for the cello, he alludes to the deep clefts that hide the Nibelungs within the earth.

| Smith Ex 11: | iii, 200; | Vc. | Mime: This wretch compels us to slip into chasms. |
| Smith Ex 12: | iii, 417; | Vc. | Alberich: Just what do you want down here? |

Smith Ex 13:	Int. 3, 25;	Vc.	Discussed in Int. 3 analysis.
Smith Ex 14:	iv, 69;	Vc.	Alberich: Alright! The Nibelungs will come (out from the clefts) at my call.
Smith Ex 15:	iv, 81;	Vc.	The Nibelungs emerge from the cleft.

The viola plays the Nibelung smiths motive five times.

Smith Ex 16:	iii, 237;	Br.	Mime: He treats me most cruelly, I did as told, forged him a helm. He told me in detail how ...
Smith Ex 17:	iii, 656;	Br.	Loge: Yet, let me warn you . . .
Smith Ex 18:	iii, 680;	Br.	Loge: ... if a thief slipped in while you slept...
Smith Ex 19:	Int. 3, 23;	Br.	Discussed in Int. 3 analysis.
Smith Ex 20:	iv, 514;	Br.	Loge: The hoard is spent.

As he does with the Ring motive, Wagner uses the viola to represent denial. In Example 16, Mime laments his unfair treatment by Alberich, as he was given the job of forging the helm, but denied payment for his work. In the next two examples, Loge advises Alberich not to take absolute control, as that would certainly incite a thief to steal his ring. Note that in this passage the viola alternates with a horn scoring of the motive (Example 7), asking us to consider the qualities of fairness and restraint in dealing wisely with power. In the last example, Loge indicates to the giants that the gods have forfeited the entire hoard in response to the giants' request for more gold.

In the related combination of horn and viola, Wagner expresses the idea of distrust.

Smith Ex 21:	iii, 413;	Hn, Br.	Alberich watches Loge distrustfully.
Smith Ex 22:	iv, 485;	Hn, Br.	Loge: Away, you rude one! Fafner: Add more!

In Example 22, Fafner tries to make sure that Loge is giving him a fair amount of gold, while Loge tries to spread the gold as thinly as possible.

Wagner uses the combination of cello and double bass to represent all that is hidden in darkness.

Smith Ex 23:	iii, 127;	Vc, Cb.	Discussed in analysis of Interlude 2.
Smith Ex 24:	iii, 139;	Vc, Cb.	Loge: The glow is seen through the darkness in fiery vapors.
Smith Ex 25:	iii, 208;	Vc, Cb.	Mime: Through the golden ring, he sees in his greed where the gold is hidden. Then he must dig ...

This combination adds an even deeper level to the cello scorings of the Nibelung smiths motive, which emphasize deep isolation. There is also an interlude scoring that adds viola to the cello and bass (Int. 2, 90; Br, Vc/Vc, Cb). We will cover this in the analysis of the second interlude.

Wagner uses the tympani to add an extra element of forcefulness in some statements of the Nibelung smiths motive.

Smith Ex 26:	iii, 115;	St. Hn, Pauk.	Alberich's scoldings retreat in the distance.
Smith Ex 27:	iv, 97-124;	Various string combinations, Pauk.	Alberich commands his slaves to hurry delivering the gold to the gods.

In both examples, the tympani play an onomatopoetic role by mimicking the audible effect of Alberich striking his victims to keep them in line. Wagner often uses percussion to imitate actual sounds. In many scorings of the Renunciation of Love motive, the tympani serve as a "heartbeat" in order to complement the idea of renunciation of love. In the two following examples, the cymbal (with mallets) represents the icy malice of dictatorial command.

Smith Ex 28:	iii, 268;	Hb, Fag, Hn, Cym.	Mime: ... that I as freeman shall command!

Smith Ex 29:   iv, 114;   Ten, Btbs, Cym.   Alberich kisses his ring and
                                                stretches it out commandingly.

Example 28 is part of the statement of the Ring motive which discusses
command (See Ring motive, ex. 55). Example 29 uses tenor and bass tubas
to emphasize the agony and gloomy depression of the Nibelung race.[16]

Wagner employs a horn-bassoon combination as the basis for some of the
scorings of the Nibelung smiths motive in <u>Das Rheingold.</u> Once again, it
represents payment. Note that the first two examples are from the same
area in the fourth scene.

Smith Ex 30:   iv, 469-476;   Hn, Fag,   Loge and Froh heap up the
                                Br, BCl.   treasure between the staves.

Smith Ex 31:   iv, 479;   Hn, Fag.   Fafner presses the hoard closer
                                              together.

Smith Ex 32:   iii, 224;   Hn, Fag, Cl. Mime: To our lord we bring the
                                              hoard.

We have already been discussed the combination in Example 30. In
addition to the payment of gold reflected in the horn-bassoon combination,
the bass clarinet alludes to the power of the giants (see Ring motive, Ex.
40), as well as the horn-viola expression of distrust. In Example 31, Fafner
counts his pay as he inspects the gold ransom.

Example 32 uses a clarinet to emphasize that the Nibelungs are bringing
payment to their lord. Other related combinations are:

Smith Ex 33:   iii, 223;   Hn, Fag, Hb.   Mime: …without peace or
                                             rest …

Smith Ex 34:   iii, 227;   Hn, Cl, Hb.   Mime: … we bring the hoard.

---

[16] In his annotation to Berlioz's <u>Treatise on Instrumentation,</u> Richard Strauss asserts that
Wagner intended the tubas for just that purpose. Berlioz, Hector. <u>Treatise on
Instrumentation,</u> Rev. and Ed. by Richard Strauss, tr. by Theodore Front. (New York: E. F.
Kalmus, 1948), p. 7.

Smith Ex 35:	ii, 690;	Eng. Hn, Cl, Hn, Hb, (pizz. Vn, Br).	Loge: ... so brightly forged by the Nibelungs, servants and slaves to the ring.

We saw how Wagner scored the Ring motive with the combination of oboe, bassoon, and horn (once with clarinet) to relate to the Nibelungs' aspirations to power. Example 33 points to Mime's frustration at being a servant to Alberich.

In example 34, Mime ends his speech. The horn, clarinet, and oboe represent the gods' reaction to the Nibelungs' tragic state. In Example 35, Loge tells Fricka that she might keep Wotan from straying if she wore jewelry made from the Nibelung gold. This example uses the combination of English horn, clarinet, and horn to represent world rule (through the gold) for Valhalla.

The oboe perhaps represents the tragedy of the Nibelungs' servitude. For what seems to be a more metaphorical than musical reason, Wagner uses pizzicato upper strings to represent the twinkling of the glittering gold.

The following examples are unrelated scorings of the Nibelung smiths motive which appear only once in Das Rheingold. The first employs a violin that alternates with a viola scoring of the Nibelung smiths motive.

Smith Ex 36:	iii, 675; Vn.	Loge: Yet, what if a thief slipped in while you slept, and pulled off your ring?

Perhaps this is somehow related to the violin-viola combination in that it entails a warning to the Nibelung.

One bassoon scoring of the Nibelung smiths motive occurs in iii, 256 when Mime says, "perhaps, yes, perhaps" to his plan to overthrow Alberich. Throughout Das Rheingold, Wagner uses the bassoon to represent gloomy, murky thoughts. Perhaps this bassoon setting indicates haziness in Mime's mind. Note the use of grace notes in this example to emphasize the underhandedness of this plan.[17] In iii, 133, the bassoon is added to the double bass, but since this is a purely instrumental setting, it will be discussed in the analysis of the second interlude.

As subservient and faceless as they seem, Wagner lends depth to the smiths' characterization by scoring their leitmotive in such a variety of orchestral colors.

---

[17] Wagner uses grace notes in the low instruments at times to represent dishonesty (in this case, Alberich lurking). Four examples:

i, 31; Fag. Alberich's entrance.; iii, 106; Vc, Cb. Alberich: Here he comes—the Nibelung Lord!; i, 96; Fag, Vc, Cb. Alberich's climb.; iii, 342; Vc, Cb. Alberich drives his slaves with a whip.

The following table compares symbolic content in various scorings of the Nibelung smiths motive with those of the Ring motive.

TABLE II: COMPARISON OF RING AND SMITHS MOTIVES

Scoring	Symbol (Ring)	Symbol (Smiths)
Violin-viola	Warning	Dare
Horn	Gods of Valhalla	Fairness; justice; light.
Cello	Isolation	Subterranean clefts
Viola	Denial	Denial
Horn-Bassoon	Payment	Payment
Oboe-bassoon-horn	Nibelungs' aspiration to power.	Mime's frustration in bondage.

Of the six scorings common to both motives, the viola and horn-bassoon scorings bear identical symbolic meanings. When seen in the context of two motives, horn scoring takes on a more general reference to nobility. The cello scoring also assumes a wider range of meaning in its reference to isolation. The violin-viola scoring broadens its reference from *warning* to *dare*, and the oboe-bassoon-horn combination centers more around one character in its reference to Nibelung aspirations. Even across two motives, Wagner's scoring combinations reflect similar dramatic intent with notable regularity.

Giants motive

The Giants motive occurs fifty-four times in <u>Das Rheingold.</u> It differs from the other frequently recurring motives in that two thirds of the scorings occur in only four different combinations, while the remaining third are scored for combinations that only appear once. The clustering helps to make a strong argument for a scoring/symbolism parallel. Many statements of the motive employ a horn-bassoon combination in some capacity, indicating the principal reason for the giants' presence in the opera: payment.

The tympani scoring of the Giants motive presents an aural picture of the giants' lumbering presence.

Giant Ex 1:	ii, 47;	Pauk.	Wotan: I mind well what they (the giants) wanted.
Giant Ex 2:	iv, 351;.	Pauk	Foreshadows the giants' entrance.
Giant Ex 3:	iv, 366;	Pauk.	Loge: Fafner and Fasolt soon will be here.
Giant Ex 4:	iv, 452;	Pauk, (Vc, Cb).	The giants stick their staves in the ground in front of Freia.
Giant Ex 5:	iv, 461;	Pauk.	Wotan: Haste with the work. Really, it galls me.
Giant Ex 6:	iv, 479, 481;	Pauk.	Fafner presses the hoard closer together. Fafner: Tight and fast, fill up the gauge.
Giant Ex 7:	iv, 574;	Pauk.	Fafner: Now add the final part of the ransom.

In many of these statements, the motive itself is used as a basis for symphonic development with other motives. In Example 4 it becomes intertwined in a canonic statement of the Compact with the Giants motive that pits the horn and bassoon against the cello and bass. The scoring thus reveals the four elements of the passage: the giants, a treaty, demands,[18] and payment. Example 5 immediately precedes a viola-cello-bass setting of the Giants motive, which indicates suffering. In Example 6, the tympani alternates with cello-bass statements of the Giants motive with a superimposed horn-bassoon statement of the Nibelung Smiths motive. The total picture of the passage now includes the symbolic elements of payment, demands, giants, and smiths. Example 7 is pitted against a horn-bassoon statement of the Ring motive which emphasizes payment.

The horn statements of the Giants motive refer to the gods of Valhalla, especially Freia.

Giant Ex 8:   ii, 297;   Hn.   Fasolt: Foolishly you gods strive for
                                      Valhalla.

Giant Ex 9:   ii, 306;   Hn.   Fasolt: ... to win us a wife (Freia).

Giant Ex 10:   ii, 364;   Hn.   Fasolt (To Donner): Why interrupt us?
                                      Strife's not our choice.

Giant Ex 11:   iv, 242;   Hn.   Wotan: I hold here what sets me up —
                                      the strongest and mightiest of lords!

Giant Ex 12:   iv, 428;   Hn.   Wotan: The golden mass must first be
                                      measured.
                                      Fasolt: To lose the maiden ...

Giant Ex 13:   iv, 436;   Hn.   Fasolt: Pile the hoard in a heap so as to
                                      cover Freia's glance.

Giant Ex 14:   iv, 732;   Hn.   Fafner: More for the maid (Freia) than
                                      the gold hungered your glance.

In Example 10, the giants argue with Donner over their right to take Freia. Example 11 is immediately followed by a scoring of the Giants motive which appears once: oboe, clarinet, horn, bassoon, bass clarinet, (flute,

---

[18] see Giants motive in Vc, Cb to indicate demands.

trumpet). Since the statement appears but once in <u>Das Rheingold</u>, it is difficult to assert any symbolic interpretation.

The Giants motive rarely employs the highest pitched instruments of each orchestral family. Wagner probably used the lowered pitch to emphasize the larger-than-life quality of the giants. In doing so, it appears that he moved his symbols one notch lower in accordance with his string combinations. The Giants motive scored in the cello-bass combination thus equals the symbolic content of the viola-cello combination in any other motive. Likewise, the Giants motive scored in the viola-cello combination is equal in meaning to any other motive scored in the violin-viola combination.[19]

In the Giants motive, the combination of cello and bass is used to represent craving and demanding, ideas related to the coveting normally expressed in the viola and cello.

Giant Ex 15:	ii, 145;	Vc, Cb.	Freia: Now he's (Fasolt) coming to catch me.
Giant Ex 16:	ii, 813;	Vc, Cb, (Hn, Fag).	Fafner: Hard work went onto that fort.
Giant Ex 17:	Int. 3, 50	Vc, Cb, (Hn, Fag).	Discussed in Int. 3 analysis.
Giant Ex 18:	Int. 3, 59	Vc, Cb, (Hn, Fag, Cl).	Discussed in Int. 3 analysis.
Giant Ex 19:	Int. 3, 71	Vc, Cb, (Hn, Fag).	Discussed in Int. 3 analysis.
Giant Ex 20:	iv, 404;	Vc, Cb.	Fasolt: Stop! Don't touch her yet. Freia is still ours.

---

[19] The same ambiguity presents itself when other motives connect with the two giants. When the cello plays Freia's motive, it always refers to Fasolt, the love-struck giant. Does it refer to the characteristic loneliness implied by the cello, or does it really function as a viola, pointing to the way he has been denied the goddess?

Giant Ex 21:	iv, 478;	Vc, Cb.	Fafner presses the hoard closer together.
Giant Ex 22:	iv, 480;	Vc, Cb.	Fafner: Tight and fast, fill up the gauge.
Giant Ex 23:	iv, 501;	Vc, Cb.	Fafner: Still more this way!

In the first example, Freia cries for help as Fasolt comes lusting after her. In Das Rheingold, Fafner craves gold, but Fasolt craves the goddess. Example 16 includes a highlight in the horn and bassoon, which expresses the hidden meaning of payment. Fafner explains that he has worked hard, and now wants his wage. Example 20 occurs next to a horn-bassoon (payment) setting of the Giants motive, which illustrates the giant demanding his payment before letting Freia go. Examples 21 and 22 have already been discussed under tympani statements. The last example occurs next to a scoring of the Giants motive which occurs only once: bassoon, tympani, bass tuba. (bassoon=gloom, bass tuba=agony and frustration.) The dramatic setting has Fricka blaming Wotan for his shameful dealing while the giants demand more gold. Note the development with statements of the Nibelung smiths motive nearby. The horn setting reminds us of the gods, and the viola, because of the lowered pitch, takes the place of the violin reference to innocence and tenderness.

The viola-cello-bass combination is used to represent the hard work and suffering normally expressed by violin-viola-cello. It usually involves an instrumental highlighting to emphasize a hidden quality in the statement. In Examples 24 and 25, the giants ask for their wage. They describe the work for which they deserve Freia. The horn-bassoon complement emphasizes the payment reference.

| Giant Ex 24: | ii, 208; | Br, Vc, Cb, (Hn, Fag). | Fasolt: Mighty toil tired us not. Heavy stones were heaped by us… |
| Giant Ex 25: | ii, 526-7; | Br, Vc, Cb, (Hn, Fag). | Fafner: No more waiting! Quick, our wage! Fasolt: We've waited too long. |

In the following extended examples, Wagner uses several viola-cello-bass statements of the Giant motive. In Example 26, he uses the scoring to represent the mental battle with Wotan.

Giant Ex 26:   ii, 338-344; Br, Vc, Cb.   Fafner: I say we should carry her (Freia) off![A] Wotan:[B] Loge waits too long. Fasolt:[C] So, what shall it be? Wotan:[D] Ask another wage! Fasolt; No other.[E] Freia alone.[F] Fafner: You there, follow us!

At Point A in this section, the motive appears in the viola-cello-bass combination with the complement in the tympani. This emphasizes the giants' brute strength. Wagner superimposes the Golden Apples motive (horn) upon this, which references the goddess Freia. At Point B, all that remains is a horn-bassoon chord (D, D7) underlined by a tympani roll. The interpretation suggests Wotan searching for a way out of his trouble. Loge provides his escape. On the conscious level, Wotan transfers the blame to Loge, but in the background, on the unconscious level, the inevitable payment lurks. At Point C, the horns highlight the motive, pointing the question to Wotan, while the bassoons sustain a C major chord. We can think of the bassoons as part of the previous horn-bassoon combination, or as a reference to some haziness in the question. At Point D, the horns sustain a chord (C, C7) underlined by a viola tremolo. In relation to Point B, the horn-bassoon combination has been replaced by horns in the same pattern, showing Wotan invoking the law of Valhalla. The viola tremolo replaces the tympani, showing the mental uneasiness that underlies Wotan's might as he denies the giants their choice.[20] Point E highlights the Giants motive with tenor and bass tubas, while the horns sustain a B flat chord. The tubas point to Fasolt's frustration at being denied Freia. The horn refers to Freia herself (see Point A). At Point F, Wagner transmutes the motive to the point where the highlight is responsible for any trace of the motive in the lower strings. The highlight consists of horn and bassoon alternating with tenor and bass tubas, showing the dualism between payment and frustration. The lower strings now assume a more tremolo quality to represent the giants' growing mental anguish.

---

[20] Viola=denial.

Giant Ex 27:   ii, 798-814; Br, Vc, Cb.   AFafner and Fasolt approach.
Fafner: Hear, Wotan, our very last
words[B] Let your Freia remain here[C].
Smaller payment now will suit us.
We[D]clumsy giants want only the
[E]Nibelung's ruddy gold.
Wotan: Have you gone mad? How
can I grant you what is not mine yet,
you rascals?
[F]Fafner: Hard work[G]went into that
fort ...

In Example 27, Points A and B are almost identical, except for some
thinning in the orchestration. The horn-bassoon combination highlights
the subject of the giants' last words: payment. At Point C, we see the Ring
motive in the viola and cello, indicating coveting (see Ring motive in the Br-
Vc). A viola-cello-bass statement of the Giants motive at Point D
represents the giants' clumsiness as a handicap as the giants play for
sympathy. At Point E, all that remains of the Giants motive is the attack
with grace notes in the cello and bass. This now represents greed (see
Giants motive in the Vc-Cb), while the clarinet-bassoon scoring of the Ring
motive refers to the Nibelung (see Ring motive in the Cl-Fag.). The string
pizzicato on the word *rothes* (ruddy) possibly alludes to the dark twinkling of
the gold (see Nibelung smiths: Ex 35). At Point F, the viola-cello-bass
combination reappears with horn-bassoon highlights as Fafner describes
the toil for which he wants payment. Point G shows the motive
transformed into a partial statement of the Nibelung smiths motive.

Giant Ex 28:   iv 462-477; Br, Vc, Cb.   Freia: Help me Froh[A]! Freia's
shame[B] must be ended.[C] [D] (Loge
and Froh heap the treasure between
the staves.)

At Point A in Example 28, the viola-cello-bass combination underscores
Freia's suffering. This reflects itself in a cello scoring of the Giants motive
found at Point B. The cello is used in place of a viola scoring (denial), and
the horn accompanies this. This moment combines the symbols of
Valhalla, the hoard, sorrow, denial, and the giants. At Point C, there is a
viola-cello setting of the Giants motive, which indicates this statement as

advice or warning, in place of the usual violin-viola scoring. This is punctuated by a cello-bass pizzicato at Point D, which also touches off a symphonic development of the Nibelung smiths motive in various combinations, a canonic statement of the Compact with the Giants motive between cello-bass and tenor-bass tuba combinations, and composite statements of the Giants motive. The canon symbolizes coveting versus frustration, and the ensuing tympani, tympani-horn, and trombone combinations of the Giants motive link the symbols of force, gods, and the curse (trombone=curse). We will examine an interlude setting of the viola-cello-bass combination in the analysis of the third interlude.

The horn-bassoon combination occurs three times in Wagner's scoring of the Giants motive. Each time it occurs, it represents the idea of payment.

Giant Ex 29:	ii, 299;	Hn, Fag, (Br, Vc, Cb).	Fasolt: . . . which sits on the mountain in pledge for woman.
Giant Ex 30:	iv, 407;	Hn, Fag, (Vc, Cb).	Fasolt: Freia is still ours.
Giant Ex 31:	iv, 778;	Hn, Fag, (Str.).	Loge: ... for your foemen, see, murder their friends for the gold you have yielded.

Example 29 refers to the toil that built Valhalla, for which the Giants want payment. The viola-cello-bass complement emphasizes the toil, the horn-bassoon combination expresses payment. Example 30 refers to Freia as nothing more than an object of payment. The cello-bass combination used in place of viola-cello underlines the greed with which the giants hold on to her. The last example shows how Wotan has profited by yielding the ring. The full string accompaniment, representing anger (see Sorrow motive in the strings), includes a viola tremolo, which highlights the insanity of the murder (see article on tremolo).

There are three miscellaneous bassoon scorings of the Giants motive, all of which bear a reference to gloom.

Giant Ex 32:	iv, 727, 729;	Fag, Pauk, Btb.	Fasolt (to Fafner): Halt, greedy one! Give me some too. Justice in sharing befits us both.
Giant Ex 33:	iv, 489;	Fag, St. Horn.	Wotan: Deep is the shame burning my breast.

The bassoon-tympani-bass tuba combination appears as a counterpart to the Nibelung smiths motive in the horn. Perhaps Wagner is weighing a choice between justice and gloom symbols. The second example utilizes stopped horn to represent the insult of shame within Wotan. A third bassoon setting has already been discussed in Example 23.

Three miscellaneous string scorings occur in the second scene.

Giant Ex 34:	ii, 192-196	Str, CBT, (Pos, CBP, Pauk, BTr)	Freia: Rescue me, Froh! Fricka: Through their wicked deal, they betray you. (The two giants enter.)
Giant Ex 35:	ii, 221;	Str, (Pos, CBP, CBT).	Fasolt: Enter in, but pay our wage.
Giant Ex 36:	ii, 303;	Br, Vc, (Hn, Fag).	Fasolt: We dullards drudge away ... to win us a wife.

In Example 34, Wagner only hints at the motive, but never actually states it. Toward the end of the example, the motive is unveiled in the full strings, tympani, and contrabass tuba as the giants enter. The bass trumpet, trombone, and contrabass trombone highlight this. This scoring, while it could conceivably harbor symbolic references to the curse of the ring, seems to be purely coloristic, as Wagner wishes to impress us with the stature of the giants upon their first entrance. Example 35 appears with a highlight comprised of trombone, contrabass trombone, and contrabass tuba to hint at the real wage they will receive for their work: death.

Example 36 is a viola-cello scoring of the Giants motive highlighted by a horn-bassoon combination which hints at the giants' growing restlessness at not being paid. The giants are warning Wotan to pay them before they lose patience. The viola and cello take the place of the normal violin-viola reference to warning; the horn-bassoon combination refers to payment.

There is one additional scoring of the Giants motive in <u>Das Rheingold</u>—trombone and contrabass trombone (ii, 348; Pos, CBP). It may have some symbolic meaning with regard to the curse, but since it is an incomplete statement, and appears only once, we cannot draw any firm conclusion.

Many of the scorings used in statements of the Giants motive appear in statements of other motives. The following table compares the symbolic content found in scorings of the Giants motive common with those of the Ring motive and the Nibelung Smiths motive.

TABLE III: COMPARISON OF RING, SMITHS, AND GIANTS MOTIVES

Scoring	Giants	Smiths	Ring
Tympani	Giants' presence	Force	---
Horn	Gods of Valhalla; Freia	Fairness; Justice	Gods of Valhalla; Fairness; Light
Cello-Bass*	Craving	———	Coveting
Horn-Bassoon	Payment	Payment	Payment
Viola-Cello*	Warning	Dare	Warning

In both motives where it appears, the tympani takes on an onomatopoetic reference even though its meaning is different in either case. While the horn, and the two string combinations are fairly consistent among the three motives, only the horn-bassoon combination bears exactly the same symbolic meaning in all three cases.

The giants are simple, fairly straightforward characters in Das Rheingold. Wagner allows us further insight into their natures by "painting" them with a variety of orchestral colors.

* The scorings of the Ring and Smiths motives have been adjusted in accordance with the lowered pitch of the Giants motive string scorings.

Sorrow motive

The Sorrow motive is a simple, yet moving expression of sighing sadness. It is perhaps the most difficult leitmotive in <u>Das Rheingold</u> to identify, as it can consist melodically of nothing more than a descending semi-tone, and harmonically of nothing more than the resolution of a fully diminished seventh chord. Thus, what may appear to be a statement of the Sorrow motive may occur in passages having nothing whatsoever to do with sorrow. It is inconceivable that Wagner meant every descending semi-tone in <u>Das Rheingold</u> to convey the intensity of feeling found in a full statement of a leitmotive. Therefore, we must determine which descending semi-tones are meant as motivic statements, and which are not. The problem becomes further complicated by the fact that certain partial or transmuted statements of other motives tend to masquerade as statements of the Sorrow motive, most notably the motives that indicate Greeting to the Rheingold and Renunciation of Love. After considering which descending semi-tones are really free material or transmuted statements of other motives, we find sixty-three actual statements of the Sorrow motive.

After identifying true motivic statements, we need to assess which instruments actually play the motive. At times, sustaining instruments underscore a statement of the motive by matching its rhythm. They provide a harmonic part of the statement, even though these instruments fail to meet the harmonic and/or melodic criteria normally required of instruments comprising a statement of the Sorrow motive. They must be considered a part of the scoring combination since one hears them as part of the chord which accompanies the descending semi-tone.

In the article on the Ring motive, we saw how Wagner's clarinet-bass clarinet-bassoon scoring made reference to hate. When this combination plays the Sorrow motive, a character expresses distaste at that which was formerly attractive.

Sorrow Ex 1:	ii, 909;	Cl, BCl, Fag.	Loge: Can (Fricka) be grieving at Wotan's gloomy decline that makes him suddenly old?
Sorrow Ex 2:	ii, 146;	Hb, Cl, BCl, Fag.	Alberich: . . . who gleams less brightly and looks too slick?
Sorrow Ex 3:	Int. 2, 28;	Hb, Eng. Hn, Cl, BCl, Vc.	Discussed in Int. 2 analysis.
Sorrow Ex 4:	iii, 375;	Eng. Hn, Cl, BCl, Fag.	Alberich: If any be idle, Mime shall answer (to my wrath).
Sorrow Ex 5:	iii, 675;	Cl, BCl, Vc.	Loge: Your slaves tremble with fear. Yet, what if a thief …
Sorrow Ex 6:	iv, 311;	Cl, BCl.	Alberich: Thus urged by sorest of spite...

In Example 1, Loge comments on Fricka's growing horror upon seeing Wotan age so rapidly. In Example 2, Alberich denounces his infatuation with Woglinde in favor of her sister. Examples 3 through 6 contain related combinations which refer to the Nibelung's hatred. Example 5 references the idea that no one dare hate Alberich. The cello personifies the covert nature of the slave who might hate Alberich enough to plot against him. Example 6 uses the bass clarinet and clarinet to refer to spite.[21]

When examining the Ring motive, we saw how Wagner used the English horn-clarinet-bassoon combination to convey the idea of world rule for Alberich. The following similar scorings of the Sorrow motive express the sadness of a world ruled by the dwarf.

Sorrow Ex 7:	iv, 85;	Eng. Hn, Cl, (Fag).	The Nibelungs ascend with Alberich's treasure.
Sorrow Ex 8	iv, 93;	Eng. Hn, Cl, Fag.	Alberich: Oh, shame and disgrace, that my slaves should see me shackled.

---

[21] The Nibelung Scorn motive appears most often in the clarinets.

| Sorrow Ex 9: | iii, 312; | Hb, Eng. Hn, Cl, Fag. | Mime: There must we dig (for Alberich's gold) … |

Example 7 shows the scoring of the Sorrow motive developing into the full English horn-clarinet-bassoon statement found in Example 8. In this passage, a shackled Alberich commands his slaves to deliver all of the Nibelung hoard to the gods. In Example 9, the oboe adds a further note of tragedy as Mime relates the plight of the slaves who labor to win Alberich's riches.

There are two statements of the Sorrow motive scored in an English horn-clarinet combination. These refer to beauty. When Wagner adds the bass clarinet, a character shows lack of concern for beauty.

Sorrow Ex 10:	i, 79;	Eng. Hn, Cl.	Alberich (to Wellgunde): How bright and fair in the light you shine.
Sorrow Ex 11:	i, 187;	Eng. Hn, Cl.	Alberich: Am I not lovely, dainty and pleasant, smooth and bright?
Sorrow Ex 12:	i, 228;	Eng. Hn, Cl, BCl.	Alberich: How dull and base seems all they (the other Rheinmaidens) are …
Sorrow Ex 13:	iv, 532;	Eng. Hn, Cl, BCl.	Fasolt: Must I now lose her? (Freia)
Sorrow Ex 14:	iv, 180;	Hb, Eng. Hn, Cl.	Wotan: Ask if the Rheinmaidens gave it (the gold) to you to own.

In Examples 10 and 11, Alberich pays similar compliments to Wellgunde and to himself. In Example 12, Alberich is prepared to reject the other Rheinmaidens who were once so dear to him. Example 13 refers to this when Fasolt asks nonchalantly if Freia is now lost to him. Wagner follows this passage with a fragmented statement of the Nibelung smiths motive in the viola, which symbolizes denial. A cello statement of the Hoard motive underscores this, and a sustained note in the horn sounds as Fasolt decides to examine the size of the ransom by himself. The cello symbolizes Fasolt acting on his own, and the horn symbolizes Freia. In Example 14, Wagner adds the oboe to the English horn-clarinet combination, as Wotan refers to the tragic outcome of Alberich's courtship.

The combination of cello and double bass appears five times in Wagner's scoring of the Sorrow motive. This scoring makes a reference to hiding in the darkness.

Sorrow Ex 15:	iii, 322;	Vc, Cb.	Hearing Alberich approach, Mime crouches down.
Sorrow Ex 16:	iii, 334;	Vc, Cb.	Alberich: Now here! Now there! Hehe! Hoho! Lazy bunch!
Sorrow Ex 17:	iii, 436;	Vc, Cb.	Loge: You cowered once within a cold hole. Where were your light and fire?
Sorrow Ex 18:	iii, 794;	Vc, Cb.	Loge: Can you also ... (grow smaller?)
Sorrow Ex 19:	iv, 33;	Vc, Cb, (Vn, Br).	Loge: For vengeance to help you, you must first talk yourself free.

In Example 15, Mime crouches down into the darkness upon hearing Alberich's approach. Alberich yells at his slaves as he approaches in Example 16. In Example 17, the reference to darkness is more indirect, as Loge refers to a cold hole, which we must assume is also dark, since he asks Alberich about his absence of light. This is a good example of Wagner's use of a particular repeated scoring in order to emphasize certain subtleties in the text. Example 18 foreshadows Loge's next line: "That is the best way to hide from dangerous foes." Perhaps the answer to this, found in the English horn and bassoon, hints at Alberich's real fear of being captured by the gods, but since this is the only statement of this combination, we cannot assume any symbolic content. In Example 19, Wagner highlights the cello-bass combination with a statement of the Sorrow motive in the violin and viola. Loge advises Alberich that the gods are not threatened by the

Nibelung's angry statements. The violin-viola combination refers to advice (or possibly to the Nibelung's threats) and the cello-bass combination indicates Loge dismissing Alberich to the same dark, ineffectual hole that he lay in prior to Loge's support.

Four statements of the Sorrow motive make prominent use of the tubas. As previously discussed, the tubas refer to the agony of the Nibelungs.

Sorrow Ex 20:	Int. 1, 34;	Tbs.	Discussed in Int. 1 analysis.
Sorrow Ex 21:	iii, 413;	Fag, CBT.	The Nibelungs slip off into the gloom.
Sorrow Ex 22:	Int. 3, 23;	BTb, CBT.	Discussed in Int. 3 analysis.
Sorrow Ex 22:	iv, 93;	TTb, BTb.	Alberich: Oh shame and disgrace!

In Example 21, the contrabass tuba combines with the bassoon to produce a reference to gloom along with the reference to agony. In Example 23, Alberich expresses his own agony.

The Sorrow motive is scored four times for the oboe. As mentioned earlier, Wagner used the oboe to represent naïveté and tragedy. In three instances, Wagner personifies these qualities in the character of Mime.

Sorrow Ex 24:	iii, 12;	Hb, Vc.	Mime: Let me alone.
Sorrow Ex 25:	iii, 139;	Hb.	Mime: Ow! Ow!
Sorrow Ex 26:	iii, 143;	Hb.	Wotan: What lies on the stones?
Sorrow Ex 27:	iv, 708;	Hb.	Wotan throws the ring on the pile.

In Example 24, the cello plays with the oboe, strengthening the reference to Mime's request to be left alone. In Example 26, the object which lies on the stones is Mime. Example 27 refers to Wotan sadly giving up the ring.

There are two examples of a bassoon-double bass scoring of the Sorrow motive.

Sorrow Ex 28:   i, 96;   Fag,Cb.   Alberich climbs with difficulty.

Sorrow Ex 29:   iii, 1;   Fag, Cb.   Alberich enters, dragging the shrieking Mime.

These two examples present Alberich in two opposite situations. In both examples, the meter changes to $\frac{2}{4}$, and the surrounding orchestration is almost identical. In fact, the only real difference between these two scorings is that the first is in E minor and the second is in Bb minor, a tritone away.[22] There is a related scoring which adds a cello (Int. 2, 83; Fag, Vc, Cb.), but this occurs in an interlude, so it will be discussed in the analysis of Interlude 2.

The Sorrow motive is scored three times for the combination of violin and viola. Each of these scorings refers to the way Alberich has enslaved his people through punishment and threat.

Sorrow Ex 30:   iii, 80;   Vn, Br.   Alberich (after beating Mime): I thank you, numbskull! Your work is tried and true.

Sorrow Ex 31:   iii, 208;   Vn, Br.   Mime:. . . he sees . . . where the gold is hidden. (Then we must seek it.)

Sorrow Ex 32:   iii, 344;   Vn, Br.   Alberich threatens his slaves.

Example 30 shows a sarcastic Alberich who has just struck his brother. In Example 31, Mime explains how the Nibelungs came to be slaves of Alberich.

Four full string settings of the Sorrow motive appear in <u>Das Rheingold</u>. Each of these settings indicates great anger welling up in a character's speech.

---

[22] Wagner was fond of using literal devices to show contrast, as evidenced by his use of Db major to portray Valhalla, and his use of the relative minor (Bb minor) to portray the gloom of Nibelheim.

Sorrow Ex 33:	i, 275;	Str.	Alberich: Alas; Alas! The third one so dear (betrays me as well?)
Sorrow Ex 34:	Int. 3, 105;	Str.	Discussed in Int. 3 analysis.
Sorrow Ex 35:	iv, 169;	Str.	Wotan: Shameless elf, do you rave (to claim you own the ring?)
Sorrow Ex 36:	iv, 209;	Str.	Alberich: (The ring) is a toy for prince's amusement. Shall peace be your prize for my curse?

In Example 33, Alberich is finally frustrated with his effort to court the Rheinmaidens, as the third and last maiden refuses him. Wotan's first statement of true anger in his argument with Alberich appears in Example 35. In Example 36, the string accompaniment to Alberich's rage builds into an agitated tremolo, and finally gives way to a horn-bassoon-bass clarinet statement of the Ring motive, signifying a threat to Wotan.

Wagner uses the clarinet-bassoon combination three times to score the Sorrow motive. Similar to Ring motive statements, the combination refers to the Nibelungs.

Sorrow Ex 37:	i, 265;	Cl, Fag.	Flosshilde (to Alberich): . . .to see and hear nothing but you.
Sorrow Ex 38:	iii, 4;	Cl, Fag.	Alberich (to Mime): Rascally dwarf!
Sorrow Ex 39:	iii, 183;	Cl, Fag.	Mime: . . . the Nibelungs' downtrodden host.

In other motives, we saw how the combination of oboe-bassoon-horn (sometimes with clarinet) relates to the idea of the Nibelung's aspirations to power. This scoring occurs twice in expressing the Sorrow motive, and it carries the same meaning.

| Sorrow Ex 40: | iii, 88; | Hb, Fag, Hn, Cl. | Alberich: Hoho! (Bow down to the Nibelung lord.) |

| Sorrow Ex 41: | iv, 304; | Hb, Fag, Hn, Cl, BCl. | Alberich: The ring's lord as the ring's slave (till I recapture the ring). |

A scoring found twice in <u>Das Rheingold</u> adds an English horn to the oboe-bassoon-horn-clarinet combination. Both scorings refer to an obstacle in the path of power.

| Sorrow Ex 42: | i, 275; | Hb, Fag, Hn, Cl, Eng. Hn. | Alberich: Alas! The third one (so dear) ... |
| Sorrow Ex 43: | iv, 118; | Hb, Fag, Hn, Cl, Eng. Hn, (Pos). | The Nibelungs run back into the clefts. |

In Example 42, Alberich has been thwarted by the third of his love objects before finding the fourth in the form of gold. Example 43 refers to this when Alberich's slaves retreat after forfeiting the hoard to the gods. Alberich thinks his torment is finally over until the gods demand the final part of his wealth—the ring. At the end of this statement, the trombones play the Sorrow motive, possibly foreshadowing the Nibelung's curse.

Statements of the Sorrow motive appear twice scored for the combination of violin-viola-cello. When this scoring appears, it makes reference to toil and labor. In these two statements, Mime is the one who toils.

| Sorrow Ex 44: | iii, 13; | Vn, Br, Vc. | Mime: My toil and sweat molded the work. |
| Sorrow Ex 45: | iii, 143; | Vn, Br, Vc. | Mime (crouched in pain): Ow! Ow!... Leave me in peace. |

Example 45 refers back to Example 45, as these two excerpts are from Mime's first two long speeches, both of which, to a large extent, are accompanied by violin, viola, and cello.

A horn setting of the Sorrow motive appears twice. Each time, it refers to Freia. This godly reference is consistent with horn scorings of other motives.

Sorrow Ex 46: iv, 394; Hn.   Froh: (Freia gives us) … youth that is endless in joy.

Sorrow Ex 47: iv, 463; Hn.   Froh: Freia's shame must now be ended.

A related scoring appears toward the end of the third scene when Loge sarcastically expresses amazement at Alberich's boasts of power. The oboe adds a hint of pity to Loge's remark.

Sorrow Ex 48: iii, 736; Hb, Hn.   Loge: This work without equal I cannot believe.

In the two following examples, the English horn plays the Sorrow motive. Each time, it refers to Alberich's imprisonment by the gods.

Sorrow Ex 49: iii, 832; Eng. Hn.   Loge: There—the toad! Capture him quick!

Sorrow Ex 50: iv, 81; Eng. Hn.   Wotan: (We won't untie you) ... until all has been paid.

In Example 49, Alberich has changed into a toad. As soon as he does this, Loge and Wotan tie him up. In Example 50, Wotan addresses a shackled Alberich, as he states the condition for Alberich's release.

The following are examples of combinations that appear once in Wagner's scoring of the Sorrow motive. Many of them are related to scorings previously discussed.

Two scorings which feature the trombones prominently can be found in the beginning of the third scene. These will be discussed in the analysis of Interlude 2.

One scoring uses solo violin and flute to project a mood of lightness and tenderness.

Sorrow Ex 51: i, 209; Solo Vn, Fl.   Flosshilde: Sweetest balm, surely her love would bring.

Wagner combines the bassoon and cello in the following scoring of the Sorrow motive.

Sorrow Ex 52:   ii, 564;   Fag, Vc.   Loge: Many have I asked…

This statement from Loge's narrative will be discussed in the context of the full analysis of the narrative.

Three scorings of the Sorrow motive feature prominent tremolo strings. This sonority represents mental unrest or agitation.

Sorrow Ex 53:	ii, 912;	Br, trem. Vc.	Fricka: Woe's me! Woe's me! What has gone wrong?
Sorrow Ex 54:	iii, 561;	Vc, Cb, Hb, Fag, Vn, Br trem.	Alberich: All things that live, too shall forswear it (love). Ensnared by my gold ...
Sorrow Ex 55:	iv, 195;	Cb, Eng. Hn, trem. Vn, Br, Vc.	Alberich: (The gods would have robbed the Rheingold had it been as easy to forge) as to steal.

In Example 53, the gods are trapped in a fog represented by tremolo cello that symbolizes the characters' private exclamations of horror. The viola perhaps foreshadows the element of denial found in Loge's unsolicited answer to Fricka's question: "I have it; Learn what you're lacking." Example 54 uses the double reed combination oboe-bassoon, which relates to the Nibelungs' aspirations to power. The underlying cello-bass combination makes a reference to those ensnared by Alberich's dark power. The tremolo violin-viola combination refers to the insanity of Alberich's warning. In Example 55, the tremolo violin-viola-cello combination refers to Alberich's mental uneasiness as be describes the toil of forging the ring. The English horn reminds us of his present state of bondage, and the double bass perhaps represents a note of darkness.

In the Ring motive, we saw that the horn-bassoon-bass clarinet combination refers to threats to Wotan. One such combination comprises a statement of the Sorrow motive in the third scene (iii, 227) when Loge explains why Alberich threatens Mime.

There is one example in which the Sorrow motive is scored for stopped horn. It appears in the first scene when the three Rheinmaidens reject Alberich by laughing at him.[23] The stopped horn, in this case, refers to insult.

Wagner scores the Sorrow motive as an orchestral tutti three times in the fourth scene.

Sorrow Ex 56:	iv, 64;	Hb, Eng, Hn, Cl, BCl, Fag, CBT.	Alberich kisses his ring.
Sorrow Ex 57:	iv, 323;	Str., WW, (Pos, Btr, CBT).	Alberich: You cannot flee from my curse. (Disappears into the cleft.)
Sorrow Ex 58:	iv, 584-590		Fasolt: Freia is ours forever.[A] Freia: Help me! Fricka: Haughty god! Give them their way. Froh:[B] Spare not the gold. Donner: Give them the ring.[C]

Wagner probably intended these orchestral tutti to have a coloristic meaning. Some symbols are, however, present. In Example 56, we see the woodwind scoring noted in Examples 42 and 43 that signifies an obstacle in the path of power. Wagner adds a tuba, which represents agony. There is a direct bearing on the storyline at this point, since Alberich is kissing his ring in order to forfeit gold to the gods, a moment that marks a great obstacle in his quest for world rule. The enormous tutti found in Example 57 dissolves into a scoring for five low instruments as Alberich disappears into the cleft: contrabass tuba, trombone, bass clarinet, bassoon, and double bass. It seems appropriate that these instruments should join in this statement, as their symbolic meanings are, respectively; agony, curse, scorn, gloom, and darkness, In the extended Example 58, the motive is scored three different

---

[23] i, 266. See article on stopped horn.

ways. At point A, it is played by a woodwind combination that represents obstacles in the way of power, with added tremolo upper strings, representing mental anguish. At point B, the strings are replaced by the horn, representing fairness and godliness, as Froh advises Wotan to forfeit all the gold. At point C, Wagner adds tremolo upper strings, along with flute and double bass. The upper strings refer once again to mental anguish, and the flute represents the lightness with which Donner intended his remark. The bass underscores the flute as an indication of the true darkness of this statement. This moment is indeed an obstacle for the gods, as they are now forced to relinquish the ring. The subtly changing scorings help to emphasize all aspects of the moment.

Sorrow is a prevalent motive in <u>Das Rheingold</u>. By linking the basic idea of the motive with so many different orchestral colors, Wagner is able to express many different gradations of the emotion. Symbolism found in several of these scorings correlates strongly with statements of other widespread motives.

The following table compares symbolic contextual meanings of all scorings of the Sorrow motive shared with either the Ring motive, Smiths motive, or the Giants motive.

TABLE IV: COMPARISON OF RING, SMITHS, GIANTS, AND SORROW MOTIVES

Scoring	Sorrow	Ring	Smiths	Giants
Cl, BCl, Fag	Distaste	Hate		
Eng. Hn., Cl, Fag	Nibelung rule	Nibelung rule		
Vc, Cb	Darkness	Darkness		
Tbs	Agony	Agony		
Vn, Br	Punishment	Warning	Dare	Warning*
Cl, Fag	Nibelungs	Nibelungs		
Hb, Fag, Cl, Hn	Nibelungs' aspirations	Nibelungs' aspirations	Mime's frustration in bondage	
Vn, Br, Vc	Toil			Hard work*
Hn	Freia	Gods of Valhalla	Fairness	Gods of Valhalla; Freia
Pos	Curse	Curse		

Two scorings are common to all four motives: horn, and violin-viola. The horn is consistently associated with godliness, nobility and fairness. The violin-viola combination takes on a more general meaning of *threat*. Shared by three of the motives, the oboe-bassoon-horn-clarinet combination remains fairly constant as an indicator of Nibelung aspirations. The symbols common to two motives are consistent in their meaning.

* Adjusted to accommodate commonly pitched string symbols in the Giants motive.

Valhalla motive

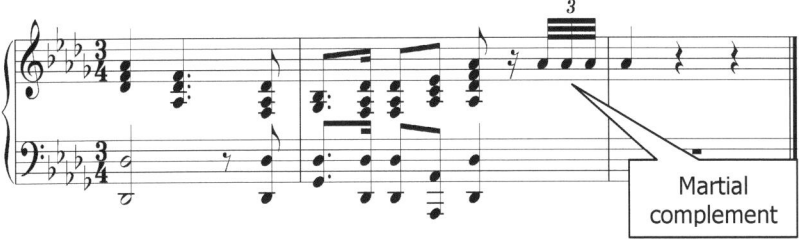

The Valhalla motive is the only motive in Das Rheingold that is also the basis of an orchestral piece in and of itself. The first statement of the motive appears in the prelude to scene two which is composed entirely of motivic statements. The motive is comprised of two parts: melody and martial complement. The orchestration of the prelude is comprised of trumpet, bass trumpet, trombone, contrabass trombone, and tubas.

Here is a summary of the orchestral shading of the first nineteen bars (up to *a tempo*):

Bar #	Melody	Complement
1-6	Tbs, CBP	Tr, Pos
7-8	Tbs, CBP, BTr	Tr, Pos
9-10	Tr, BTr, Pos, Tbs, CBP	Tr, Pos
11-12	Tr, BTr, Pos, CBt, CBP	Tr, BTr
13-14	Tr, Tbs, CBP	Tr, Pos
15-19	Tr, BTr, Pos, Tbs, CBP	Tr, Pos

It seems strange that Wagner would use a full brass choir without horns, especially since horn scorings of other motives generally refer to the gods of Valhalla. Instead, he used the tubas, which generally refer to agony and depression. This would suggest that Wagner intended the opening portrait of Valhalla to be one which is splendid but foreshadows gloom. The surrounding complement, made up of trumpet, bass trumpet, and trombone, indicates curse alternating with victory, and foreshadows the fate of Valhalla at the end of <u>Das Rheingold</u>[24].

There are two other large brass scorings which include almost identical development of the motive.

Valhall Ex 1:   ii, 16-34.   Wotan: The eternal work is conceived. On mountain summit, the gods' abode. Proudly stand the glittering walls. As I planned in my dream; Just the way I desired I Strong and fair, see how it looms. Lofty, lordly abode!

Valhall Ex 2:   iv, 873-895.   Wotan: As it sets, the sun's bright eye glows, its glorious gleam gilds tower and wall. In the morning's radiance, bravely it glistens, lying lordless there, proudly luring my feet.

Example 2 includes in it a four-measure insert which uses the horn as a complement when Wotan speaks of the tower's similarity to his dream. Afterwards, the statement continues in the same manner as in the overture. A shorter, similar brass scoring occurs when Wotan speaks of his urge to spread his dominion instead of staying in Valhalla. The full string scoring following this refers to his indignation at the thought of being held prisoner in his own palace[25].

Valhall Ex 3:   ii, 100-108.   Wotan: You must yet grant to my godhood that, in the castle's confines still may I conquer the world that's without. Wandering and change are loved by all. I too must have some amusement.

The epilogue to <u>Das Rheingold</u> is a twenty-two-bar full orchestral tutti used for coloristic purposes which expands this general brass development.

---

[24] In statements of the Rheingold motive, the combination trumpet-bass trumpet indicates victory, while the trumpet alone refers to celebration, and the bass trumpet alone refers to dormancy.

[25] See article on Sorrow motive in the strings.

Three statements of the Valhalla motive are scored for horn and bassoon. As was the case in other motives, each of these refers to payment.

Valhall Ex 4:	ii, 437;	Hn, Fag, Trem. Vn, Br, Vc, (Cl, Eng. Hn).	Loge: Roof and court, tower and hall, that blessed abode, it now stands. I checked the lordly walls myself, and all was sound, perfectly made. Fafner and Fasolt kept to their word.
Valhall Ex 5:	ii, 814;	Hn, Fag.	Fafner: (Hard work) made that fort.
Valhall Ex 6:	iv, 800;	Hn, (Hb, Eng. Hn); Hn, Fag, (Hb, Eng. Hn, Cl).	Fricka:[A] . . . your noble castle gleams, [B]Now, it awaits with shelter.

In Example 4, Loge speaks to Wotan about the giants' payment. The tremolo violin-viola-cello underscoring refers to the toil that built the dreamlike hall.[26]   As Loge expounds upon the beauty of the hall, the English horn and clarinet play the complement to the motive.[27] In Example 5, Fafner demands his payment. Example 6 begins with a horn statement of the Valhalla motive at Point A, which refers to Valhalla as the gods' home. At Point B, the horn-bassoon statement enters, showing Wotan's thoughts turning toward the price of the hall. The oboe-English horn-clarinet complement refers to the innocence and beauty of the hall.

Wagner scores the Valhalla motive for the horn three times. As seen in other motives, horn scorings refer to the godly aspect of Valhalla.

| Valhall Ex 7: | ii, 88; | (Hn). | Fricka: . . . tarry at home. |
| Valhall Ex 8: | ii, 418; | Hn. | Loge: ... bargained with the giants that time? |

---

[26] See article on string tremolo.

[27] Eng. Hn, Cl = beauty. See article on Sorrow motive.

Valhall Ex 9:	iv, 933-945;	Hn, (Tr); various.	Fricka:[A] What means the name? I've never heard you name it. Wotan: What my spirit[B] has found to master my dread[C] when triumph is won, now[D] makes the meaning clear.
Valhall Ex 10:	iii, 641;	Hb, Hn.	Loge: I must hail you (Alberich) as mightiest.
Valhall Ex 11	iv, 994;	Hb, Hn, (Pauk).	Loge: Instead, enjoy the brave new gleam that comes from the gods.

In Example 7, the complement alone is played, reinforcing Fricka's urge to convince Wotan to stay at Valhalla. In Example 8, Loge refers to the compact with the giants who built the home. Loge's next statement tells of his aversion to domestic life. Perhaps to show the contrast, Wagner punctuates this sentence with a statement of the Valhalla motive scored in the clarinet and bassoon, a combination used to represent the antithesis of the gods, the Nibelungs.

Example 9 is an extended portion taken from near the end of the opera. At Point A, Wotan has just named his palace Valhalla, and invited Fricka to live there with him. The horn signifies Valhalla as the gods' home, and the trumpet, which plays the complement to the motive, signifies celebration. At Point B, Wotan talks about the spirit which masters his dread. A new statement of the motive enters at this point which, by Point C, develops into an oboe-bassoon-horn-clarinet-tenor tuba scoring with trumpet-bass trumpet-tympani complement. The interpretation of this scoring shows that the Nibelungs' aspirations to power and agony of servitude are now reflected onto Wotan, since he, like Alberich, was forcibly stripped of his ring. The complement contains symbols of victory and force, referring to the battle already won. At Point D, the statement dissolves into an orchestral tutti. The subtext indicates that even though Wotan now shares the same fate as Alberich, the beauty and security of the hall consoles him. A similar development of the horn statement occurs at the beginning of the epilogue. Examples 10 and 11 add the oboe to taint the majesty of command with a hint of tragedy.

Wagner scored five statements of the Valhalla motive for oboe-bassoon-horn-(clarinet) combination. As with other motives, combinations of this nature refer to the Nibelungs' aspirations to power.

Valhall Ex 12:	iii, 619;	Hb, Fag, Hn, Str, Fl.	Alberich: The Nibelung hoard shall rise!
Valhall Ex 13:	iii, 651;	Hb, Fag, Hn, Cl, Fl, KlF.	Loge: They too must be your (Alberich's) slaves.
Valhall Ex 14:	iii, 793,	Hb, Fag, Hn, Cl.	Loge: I confess to the wonder (of Alberich's might).

Example 12 uses strings to refer to Alberich's anger. The flute serves as the end of a woodwind development. Example 13 uses flute and piccolo to mock Alberich, as Loge speaks sarcastically.[28]

There are two statements of a horn-cello scoring. They both refer to Wotan's private dream of paradise.

Valhall Ex 15:	ii, 7;	Hn, Vc, (Tr, BTr).	Wotan: Manhood's honor, infinite might, towers to endless renown.
Valhall Ex 16:	iii, 577;	Hn, Vc, (Cl).	Alberich: On glorious heights, in exquisite raptures, rock yourselves!

In Example 15, Wotan salutes his new palace. The trumpet-bass trumpet complement refers to *victory*. In Example 16, the clarinet replaces the brass complement, indicating Alberich's scorn for Wotan's dream.

---

[28] iv, 332. KlF=mocking. Most statements of the Arrogance motive include piccolo to make reference to mocking.

Two string scorings occur once each. The first uses viola-cello to refer to Loge,[29] and the second uses violin-viola-cello to refer to the suffering of the Rheinmaidens.

Valhall Ex 17:	ii, 154;	Br, Vc.	Fricka: Yet, you trust him (Loge) again. Wotan: I ask no one. But where guile (is necessary)...
Valhall Ex 18:	iv, 983;	Vn, Br, Vc, (Pauk).	Loge: You in the water! Why do you wail?

We find a scoring for tubas followed by trombones in the second scene when Fasolt shows Wotan that the work has been completed.

Valhall Ex 19:	ii, 213; Tbas/Pos.	Fasolt: There stands what we built you, shimmering bright in the light of day.

This represents the first instance in Wotan's relationship with Valhalla that he realizes there is a dark side to the shining palace.

Although not as pervasive a motive as the previous four, the Valhalla motive takes on a variety of connotations, indicated by Wagner's skillful use of orchestral color. The following table demonstrates the consistency of scoring choice vs. dramatic meaning as seen in five motives.

---

[29] Many statements of Loge's motive are scored in the Br, Vc combination.

TABLE V: SCORINGS OF THE VALHALLA MOTIVE SHARED BY THE RING, SMITHS, GIANTS, OR SORROW MOTIVES

Scoring	Valhalla	Ring	Smiths	Giants	Sorrow
Tbs	Agony			Agony	Agony
Hn, Fag	Payment	Payment	Payment	Payment	
Hn	Gods of Valhalla	Gods of Valhalla	Fairness	Gods of Valhalla; Freia	Freia
Hb, Fag, Hn	Nibelungs' aspiration	Nibelungs' aspiration	Mime's frustration in bondage	Nibelungs' aspiration	Nibelungs' aspiration
Br, Vc	Loge	Coveting		Craving*	
Vn, Br, Vc	Toil			Labor*	Toil

The horn and oboe-bassoon-horn scorings are used in statements of each motive listed here. Their symbolic meanings remain fairly consistent from one motive to the next. The horn-bassoon scoring is used in four out of the five motives surveyed. Its symbolism of payment remains constant. The viola-cello combination is now found to have a reference to Loge, as well as desire. The violin-viola-cello scoring used in three out of the five motives remains fairly consistent in meaning. The tubas, also used in three out of the five, bear a consistent reference to agony.

* Adjusted to accommodate commonly pitched string symbols in the Giants motive.

Renunciation of Love motive

Nur wer der Min - ne Macht ver - sagt.

Although the Renunciation of Love motive is not as significant a theme as the preceding five leitmotives, I present it in some depth to show Wagner's symbolic intent by means of onomatopoetic scoring. Tympani and cymbals represent, respectively, the pounding heart and the icy heart. In the list of statements of the Renunciation motive, I have separated the motive into two parts. There is the melody first sung by Woglinde in scene one.

Renunc. Ex 1:   i, 484; Vce, (Pauk).   Woglinde: He who the sway of love forswears, he who delight of love forbears, that man alone finds the magic.

Underscoring this melody however, is a tympani attack preceded by two grace notes. This figure is a complement to the motive, as it accompanies all but two complete statements. Onomatopoetically, it represents a heartbeat. There are several occasions when the complement appears without the main melody of the motive, in either the tympani or the cymbal. I have listed these as partial statements of the Renunciation motive, as the dramatic situation usually involves a heartbeat or renunciation of love. Thus, what appears to be a motive with only twelve statements, is in reality a motive with several partial statements as well.

Most full statements of the Renunciation motive appear in unique and unrelated scorings or in interlude scorings. This makes it difficult to extract symbolic meaning.

There are two statements of a horn-cello combination. In these two instances, the horn is a reference to the supremacy of the gold[30], and the cello refers to the isolation of its worshipper.

---

[30] All horn statements of the Rheingold motive refer to the supreme and godly nature of the gold.

Renunc. Ex 2:	i, 538;	Hn, Vc, trem. Vn, Br, (Pauk).	Alberich: If love be denied me, my cunning shall win me delight.
Renunc. Ex 3:	ii, 718;	Hn, Vc, (Pauk).	Loge: It's easy to learn by him who forswears love.

In Example 2, Alberich is about to steal the gold and renounce all love. The tremolo violin and viola refer to his agitated warnings to the Rheinmaidens. Example 3 refers to the same moment as Loge tells Wotan about the means of unleashing the power of the gold.

Several scorings of the Renunciation motive appear only once in <u>Das Rheingold</u>. Six of them are interlude scorings[31], and will be discussed in the analysis of the interludes following scenes one and three.

One full string scoring occurs without the tympani complement. As previously discussed, the string scoring is used to represent greater anger welling up in a character's speech. Here the anger is directed toward Wotan as Fricka reprimands him for dealing so lightly with Freia's life.

Renunc. Ex 4:	ii, 113; Str.	Fricka: (You gamble with contempt for) love and woman's worth.

In the fourth scene, the piccolo is used to mock Alberich's decision to renounce love as he flees, powerless, from the gods[32]. This statement appears as a highlight of an orchestral tutti, and the tympani complement is not used.

In the following example, the tenor tubas sound the motive as Alberich describes his vision of a loveless future. As previously stated, the tenor tubas refer to agony and depression.

---

[31] Int. 1, 31 Eng. Hn, Hn, (Pauk); Int. I, 33 Eng. Hn, Hn, BCl, (Pauk); Int. 3, 81 Hn.; Int. 3, 83 Hn, Fag.; Int. 3, 85 Hn, Fag, Cl, Fl; Int. 3, 87 Hn, Fag, Cl, Fl, Hb.

[32] Most statements of the Arrogance motive include piccolo to express mocking.

Renunc. Ex 5:   ii, 549; TTb, (Pauk).   Alberich: As I have forsworn all love
for good, all things too shall forswear it.

The following is a list of all statements of only the complement to the
Renunciation motive. From its initial appearance as an underscoring to the
Renunciation motive, the complement bears a dual symbolism. It imitates
the sound of a heartbeat, and is either used in this purely onomatopoetic role,
or in its contextual association with the Renunciation motive.

The following three examples are perhaps the best arguments for interpreting
the tympani as a heartbeat.

Renunc. Ex 6:   ii, 916;   (Pauk).   Donner: My hand is sunk.
Froh: My heart is stopped.

Renunc. Ex 7:   iv, 754;   (Pauk).   Fafner kills Fasolt.

Renunc. Ex 8:   ii, 964;   (Pauk).   Loge: . . . must end the godly race.

Froh says his heart is stopping, and Fasolt's heart gradually stops as he lies
dying. Loge makes reference to this as he mentions the death of the gods.

In the following two examples, the tympani hints at the concept of
renunciation of love.

Renunc. Ex 9:   ii, 664;   (Pauk).   Loge: Yet, when it is formed into a
circlet, it will grant highest power.

Renunc. Ex 10:   ii, 793;   (Pauk).   Fasolt appears half convinced of his
brother's words. The two giants
approach Wotan again.

In Example 9, Wotan learns the power of the gold once it is made into a ring.
The tympani hints at the essential element needed to unleash the power of
the ring--renunciation of love. In Example 10, Fafner tries to convince
Fasolt that gold is worth more than Freia. As Fasolt makes up his mind, the
tympani seems to repeat a nagging question within him. The tympani
changes to the grace note form used in the Giants motive as Fasolt decides to

take the gold. The passage therefore indicates, "Renounce love? We need nothing but power!"

In Examples 11 and 12, we find two identical scorings taken from two different scenes.

Renunc. Ex 11:   iii, 392;   (Pauk/Cym).   Alberich: Tremble, you pack of slaves; All obey the ring's lord.

Renunc. Ex 12:   iv, 64;   (Pauk/Cym).   Alberich, after kissing his ring, secretly murmurs a command.

Scene iii, 389-396 is made up of several odd combinations which occur after a meter change. The scoring of scene iv, 61-68 is the same, note for note. Both scorings include Alberich kissing his ring and commanding his slaves. The two percussion instruments serve to highlight Alberich's renunciation of love to gain power.

Examples 13 and 14 occur in close proximity. The complement is used in symphonic development with statements of the Sorrow motive and the Hoard motive as the downbeat of a march.

Renunc. Ex 13:   iv, 81;   (Pauk).   Wotan: . . . till all is paid. Alberich: Oh shame and disgrace, that my slaves should see me shackled.

Renunc. Ex 14:   iv, 97;   (Cym).   Alberich: Carry there as I command! (The Nibelungs march, as Alberich scolds them.)

The tympani attack changes to the cymbal as Alberich changes his attitude from self-pity to dictatorial command. The difference between the warm thump and the icy clang symbolizes the contrast between the warm heart and the cold heart.

Wagner makes the same cymbal reference in the three following examples, where the cymbal plays the complement figure to the Renunciation motive.

Renunc. Ex 15:	iii, 262;	(Cym).	Mime: I, who had once been a prisoner, as freeman should command.
Renunc. Ex 16:	iii, 322;	(Cym).	Mime crouches as Alberich approaches.
Renunc. Ex 17:	iii, 335;	(Cym).	Wotan: We'll wait your lord here.

Example 15 reveals Mime's aspiration toward dictatorship should he usurp Alberich's power. In Example 16, Mime cringes from the malicious Alberich, who has just finished beating him. In Example 17, taken from the same passage, Wotan tells Mime that he will await Alberich's return. The cymbal punctuates Alberich's entrance in the next bar, where he appears brandishing a whip.

The Renunciation of Love motive demonstrates how Wagner is able to infuse even subtle, incomplete motivic statements with symbolic subtext. The instrumental "reminders" allow us to appreciate the multi-dimensional complexity of key moments in <u>Das Rheingold</u>.

While the preceding articles have dealt with the changing scoring of particular motives, the following two articles cover specific orchestral effects. Wagner used these two effects in motivic and non-motivic contexts to emphasize subtleties in the text, or to emphasize a point present in the action.

STOPPED HORN

One of Wagner's most direct orchestral references to extra-musical ideas is found in his use of the stopped horn. This is one of two special modifications to the normal horn sound, the other being the use of the muted horn which Wagner uses to represent magic and mystery.[33] The stopped horn appears sixteen times in Das Rheingold. Its characteristic sound is sharp and unpleasant, and is used to represent scorn, insult, and shame. In most cases, the effect refers to Alberich, as in these first two appearances of the stopped horn.

St. Hn. Ex 1:   i, 169;   Wellgunde (to Alberich): Pfui! You hairy and horrible wretch!

St. Hn. Ex 2:   i, 266;   Wellgunde and Woglinde laugh at Alberich.

Since this type of treatment originally inspired Alberich to renounce love and eventually come to power, it seems logical that he would treat others in the same manner. The following nine examples illustrate this.

St. Hn. Ex 3:   iii, 109;   Alberich: . . . the Nibelung lord! (Alberich's scoldings retreat in the distance.)

St. Hn. Ex 4:   iii, 332;   Hearing Alberich approach, Mime crouches down.

St. Hn. Ex 5:   iii, 341;   Alberich: Lazy gang; There in heaps, pile up the hoard!

St. Hn. Ex 6:   iii, 494;   Alberich: Treasures to garner, treasures to bury, so serves Nibelheim's night.

---

[33] In Das Rheingold, the muted horn appears in only two contexts: the magic of the Tarnhelm, and Erda's entrance.

St. Hn. Ex 7:	iii/ 613;	Alberich: The Nibelung hoard shall rise from silent darkness.
St. Hn. Ex 8:	iii, 779;	After turning into a dragon, Alberich returns to his original form.
St. Hn. Ex 9:	iv, 236;	Alberich: Ha! Defeated! Destroyed!
St. Hn. Ex 10:	iv 262;	Alberich: Am I now free? Really free? I greet you then with freedom's first salute. (the curse)
St. Hn. Ex 11:	iv, 289;	Alberich: Care shall consume those who possess the ring, and envy gnaw those who wish they did. Each shall lust after its delights, yet no one shall find any profit there. Let its owner never be blessed, let it draw the slayer to his doom.

In the examples taken from scene three, Alberich brags of how ruthlessly and fearlessly he rules. In the examples from scene four, Alberich first expresses his own shame at being stripped of the ring. Then, he vents his own emotions by directing his curse upon the ring at his captors, the gods.

In the following four examples, Wagner uses the stopped horn to represent insult and shame in connection with the misdeeds of the gods.

St. Hn. Ex 12:	ii, 507;	Fricka (to Wotan): See what kind of a rascal you trust? Froh: Though your name's Loge, a better name's *Liar*. Donner: Accursed fire, I'll put you out!
St. Hn. Ex 13:	iv, 489;	Wotan: Deep is the shame burning my breast.
St. Hn. Ex 14:	iv, 512;	Wotan: I think Freia's covered now.
St. Hn. Ex 15:	iv, 525;	Wotan: Let the helm go also.

In Example 12, the gods gang up on Wotan and Loge because they have agreed to a dangerous bargain which puts the gods' survival on the line. Examples 13, 14, and 15 are all taken from the same passage, and all deal with Wotan's shame and his efforts to alleviate it.

In the following example, the last stopped horn scoring found in <u>Das Rheingold,</u> Loge advises Fasolt to give Fafner the hoard, and keep the ring for himself. The stopped horn scoring at this point casts the hoard in an undesirable light and serves to help Loge convince Fasolt that the ring is a wiser choice.

St. Hn. Ex 16:   iv, 741;   Loge (to Fasolt): The hoard he shall have.
                                (Keep for yourself the ring.)

Since this scoring appears so late in the opera, Wagner has built up the stopped horn's association with scorn, insult, and shame. This allows him to subtly imply the concept of distaste by using the stopped horn out of its strict connotation.

Wagner uses stopped horn sparingly in <u>Das Rheingold,</u> and he uses it to represent a limited range of concepts. This makes it very clear that Wagner's stopped horn scoring has definite direct symbolic meaning.

TREMOLO STRING COMBINATIONS

The tremolo is used in <u>Das Rheingold</u> more for extra-musical ideas than for its general sonority. Wagner uses the device as a shiver or trembling to represent great mental agitation, or to add a surreal, dream-like quality to a moment. Since what one hears in a tremolo is more the tremolo effect than the actual timbre of the instrument, Wagner relied more heavily upon the symbolism of the tremolo itself as opposed to the symbolic roles of the specific string instruments. When more than one tremolo scoring is used in a particular passage, the symbolism becomes more obvious and thus more important as the shading changes.

The viola, usually indicative of *denial*, loses most of this meaning as the tremolo becomes the most important part of its sound.

Trem. Ex 1:	i, 568; Trem. Br.	Alberich: Then hear now my curse.
Trem. Ex 2:	iii, 302; Trem. Br.	Mime rubs his back, still sore from Alberich's beatings. Wotan and Loge laugh at Mime's tale.
Trem. Ex 3:	iii, 326; Trem. Br.	Mime: Keep a sharp look. Alberich comes.
Trem. Ex 4:	iv, 518; Trem. Br.	Fafner: Her hair still shows. Toss the helm on the pile.
Trem. Ex 5:	iv, 654; Trem. Br.	Wotan (to Erda): A lofty love sounds in your words. Wait, give me more wisdom!
Trem. Ex 6:	iv, 743; Trem. Br.	Loge: Keep for yourself the ring. Fasolt: Away, you cheater, mine is the ring! I bought it for Freia's glance.

In Example 1, Alberich's mental anguish grows as he readies himself to renounce love. Examples 2 and 3 both refer to Mime's fear of his master,

Alberich. In Example 4, Fafner becomes restless in negotiating with the gods. This same feeling of nervous tension is directed toward Fafner in Example 6, where Loge arouses Fasolt to the point of seizing the ring from his brother. Example 5 can refer either to Wotan's frustration, or to the dreamlike aura that surrounds the goddess Erda.

Six scorings for tremolo violin and viola appear in <u>Das Rheingold.</u> This scoring's normal context of warning or advice becomes buried in the tremolo, but Examples 7, 9, 11, and 12 still bear some of this meaning.

Trem. Ex 7:	ii, 129; Trem. Vn, Br.	Fricka looks anxiously offstage. Fricka: Then shelter (Freia) now.
Trem. Ex 8:	ii, 388; Trem. Vn, Br.	Freia: Sorrow! Sorrow! Wotan forsakes me!
Trem. Ex 9:	iv, 113; Trem. Vn, Br.	Alberich kisses his ring and stretches it out commandingly. The Nibelungs run away.
Trem. Ex 10:	iv, 339; Trem. Vn, Br.	Alberich exits.
Trem. Ex 11:	iv, 541; Trem. Vn, Br.	Fasolt: Woe! Her glance yet shines on me. . . . And I can't part from this woman if I see only one eye.
Trem. Ex 12:	iv, 585; Trem. Vn, Br.	Fricka: Haughty god! Give them their way. Froh: Spare not the gold. Donner: Give them the ring. Wotan: Leave me in peace. The ring is mine.

In Examples 7 and 8, Fricka and Freia worry about Wotan forsaking Freia. Example 9 shows the Nibelungs running away in fright. In Example 10, Alberich, stripped of his ring, becomes just another frightened Nibelung as he too runs back into the clefts. In Example 11, Fasolt expresses great anguish at being separated from Freia, with whom he has fallen in love.

Example 12 shows Wotan growing angry with the other gods who advise him to forfeit the ring.

In the following two examples, the viola and the cello play the tremolo. A trace of the usual symbolic meanings of *coveting* or *greed* can be found in each of these scorings, but the tremolo itself which first expresses revenge, then Freia's frightened tremblings, takes precedence over the total effect.

Trem. Ex 13:	ii, 602; Trem. Br. Vc.	Loge: The Rhine's gold the robber then stole in revenge.
Trem. Ex 14:	iv, 446; Trem. Br, Vc.	Wotan: Then place the girl as gauge for the gold.

In the following eight examples, Wagner uses the violin-viola-cello combination to play the tremolo. Although these specific tremolo scorings are used to express anxiety and surrealism, examples 17, 18, 19, and 22 refer to hard work and suffering, qualities associated symbolically with this instrumental combination.

Trem. Ex 15:	i, 545; Trem. Vn, Br, Vc.	Alberich springs to a central rock before stealing the gold.
Trem. Ex 16:	ii, 171; Trem. Vn, Br, Vc.	Fricka: . . .and (Loge) leaves you alone.
Trem. Ex 17:	iv, 218; Trem. Vn, Br, Vc.	Alberich: (If I have sinned), I have sinned against myself.
Trem. Ex 18:	ii, 681; Trem. Vn, Br, Vc.	Fricka: Would the golden trinket make some glittering gear for women to wear in show? Loge: A wife would keep her husband quite true could she but win the gold so brightly forged by the Nibelungs, servants and slaves to the ring.

Trem. Ex 19:	iii, 292; Trem. Vn, Br, Vc.	Mime: While I looked, he vanished! And though I was blind, the blows he gave me were seen.
Trem. Ex 20:	iii, 702; Trem. Vn, Br, Vc.	Alberich: The helm that hides was planned by myself. The cunningest smith, Mime forged it to order. Fast it transforms me, just as I wish, to a form that is different.
Trem. Ex 21:	iv, 556; Trem. Vn, Br, Vc.	Fafner: On Wotan's finger gleams the gold of a ring.
Trem. Ex 22:	iv, 564; Trem. Vn, Br, Vc.	Wotan: What nonsense is this? I sweated to earn the ring.

Example 15 is the first appearance of a tremolo in <u>Das Rheingold.</u> Alberich has been frustrated by all three Rheinmaidens in his attempts to court them. As he ascends nearer to the gold and prepares to steal it, the Rheinmaidens shout that he has gone mad. In Example 16, Fricka plays upon Wotan's already frayed nerves as she tells him that his ally, Loge has deserted him. In Example 17, Alberich's mental tension grows to the point where he shows contempt for himself as well as for Wotan. While Examples 15-17 refer to the unrest expressed in a tremolo. Examples 18-22 refer to the surreal, dreamlike quality that the device can also portray. Example 18 refers to Fricka's dream of keeping Wotan at home by wearing Nibelung jewelry. Loge's added line about the suffering of the Nibelungs seems not to affect her as she is lost in her dreams of vanity. Examples 19 and 20 both refer to the supernatural quality of the Tarnhelm. Example 20 emphasizes this point by having the tremolo strings play the Tarnhelm motive. Examples 21 and 22 are both taken from the same passage in scene four. The two examples compare Fafner's dream of owning the ring with Wotan's aspirations.

Two tremolo settings of the cello-bass combination appear in <u>Das Rheingold.</u> Both of these scorings refer to the madness that comes with power.

Trem. Ex 23:	iii, 590; Trem. Vc, Cb.	Alberich: Take care! For when your men first serve my commands, then your proud-decked women with their scorn for love shall serve…though love be out.
Trem. Ex 24:	iv, 751; Trem. Vc, Cb.	Fafner: Now blink upon Freia's face. You'll see the ring no more.

There are three appearances of tremolo in the full strings. The normal symbolic significance of the full string scorings leans toward *anger*. Likewise, the following tremolo scorings underscore a similar burst of hostile emotion.

Trem. Ex 25:	ii, 823; Trem. Str.	Wotan: My kindness has turned you to clowns.
Trem. Ex 26:	iii, 775; Trem. Str.	Wotan: Good, you rascal! How fast the dwarf has grown into a dragon!
Trem. Ex 27:	iv, 299; Trem. pyramid to full Str.	Alberich's curse.

In Example 26, Wotan compliments Alberich on his power to change form. Underlying this act is the true anger Wotan feels toward Alberich. The string tremolo helps to bring this concealed agitation and anger into focus, even though Wotan smiles at, and humors his foe.

A tremolo cello scoring occurs only once in <u>Das Rheingold</u>.[34] It refers to the privacy normally associated with Wagner's cello scorings, and also to the tone of hatred in Fasolt's voice as the giants discuss privately how they might overthrow both Alberich and the gods.

One tremolo double bass scoring appears in the fourth scene as Erda ascends from the center of the Earth.[35] The double bass tremolo is an aural representation of the rumbling Earth cracking apart.

---

[34] ii, 643
[35] iv, 600

There are several other examples of string tremolo present in the score of Das Rheingold, but to list them all would perhaps belabor the point. Instead, I submit the following examples. These are the passages which make the most important use of several shades of tremolo.

Trem Ex 28:   ii, 437.   Loge: There stands Wotan's wish.[A] Roof and court, tower and hall, that blessed abode—it now stands firm and sound. I checked the lordly walls myself, and all was sound, perfectly made. Fasolt and Fafner kept to their word: no stone's loose in the joints.[B] Nor was I idle, like many here. He lies, who says that I was.[C] Wotan:[D] Slyly you'd soften me up; Try not to trick me. Stick to the facts as they are.

At Point A in Example 28, Loge describes the dreamlike appearance of Wotan's castle as the violin, viola, and cello sustain a tremolo statement of the Valhalla motive. At Point B, this dissolves into a viola-cello statement of the Loge motive.[36] At Point C, the tremolo viola-cello combination echoes the statement of the Loge motive. The various shadings starting at Point D are darkened with double bass as Wotan grows impatient with Loge's slick reasoning.

Trem Ex 29:   ii, 880.   Loge:[A] Alas, what's ailing the gods? Mists, do you trick me? Mocks me a dream? You've grown so withered, fearful and pale, and the bloom has fled your cheeks. The light of your eyes has been quenched.[B] Quick, my Froh, day is still dawn. From your hand, Donner, the hammer is falling! What's wrong with Fricka? Can she be grieving at Wotan's gloomy decline that makes him suddenly old? Fricka:[C] Woe's me! Woe's me! What has gone wrong? Donner: My hand is sunk! Froh: My heart has stopped.

---

[36] Loge's motive is often found scored for Br, Vc. This suggests a direct relationship between the instruments and the character.

In this example, the tremolo strings are used to represent a fog which holds the gods powerless. At Point A, the tremolo violin and viola represent the surreal mists which first threaten the gods. At Point B, the full string tremolo setting suggests that the fog is thickening, or that the gods are frustrated at their inability to conquer the fog. At Point C, the tremolo cello alone represents the fog as the gods express their private horrors at the debilitating effects of the vapors. These three distinct orchestral expressions of the fog may help a stage director serve to re-interpret an otherwise static moment in the opera.

In the following example, Alberich asserts his mad power. The changing orchestral shadings of the tremolo strings help to express his insanity as it spirals out of control.

Trem Ex 30:   iii, 93.   Alberich: (Bow down to)[A] Alberich; [B]Now he is everywhere, watching and spying. Peace and rest now have been banished. Work for your master who watches unseen, and, when you're least aware, sees all of your actions. [C]You're his slaves, now and [D]forever!

At Point A, the tremolo begins in the cello and bass to show the darkness of Alberich's very name. At Point B, a tremolo violin-viola-cello combination expresses his vision of perennial suffering. This culminates in his threat at Point C, stated by tremolo violin and viola, followed by the full string tremolo at Point D which punctuates the end of his angry outburst.

Another passage which illustrates Alberich's insanity through the use of tremolo appears later in scene three.

Trem Ex 31:   iii, 368.   Alberich: [A]From those new-found shafts, go dig out the gold. [B]You'll feel my staff, if you do not rush! If any be idle. Mime shall answer. He'll find it is hard to escape a whipping.[C]

At Point A, Alberich expresses his covetous desire for more gold as the viola and cello play the tremolo. At Point B, as the scoring adds violin, he becomes more intent on the idea of whipping those who fail to labor hard enough. Point C punctuates this this outburst with a full string tremolo.

In the following example, the tremolo is first expressed in its most literal meaning, as a tremolo cello underscores Loge's trembling at Point A. At Point B, the violin and viola play a tremolo as Loge comments on the threatening nature of the magical serpent.

Trem Ex 32: iii, 783. Loge: My trembling, surely, betrays me. You made the monstrous serpent with speed! Now that I've seen, (I confess to the wonder).

In the following example, Wotan expresses his desire to meet with Erda to learn of his fate, while Fricka tries to convince him to remain at Valhalla.

Trem Ex 33: iii, 787. Wotan: ACare and fear fetter my soul. BHow may I end them, teach me then, Erda. CTo her I must descend!
Fricka: Where tarry then, Wotan? See how your noble castle gleams?

At Point A, the tremolo cello serves to underscore Wotan's private anxiety. The viola is added to the cello scoring at Point B, showing Wotan's frenzied desire to gain wisdom. At Point C, (on the word *Erda*) the tremolo violin and viola enter, referring to the advice of the Earth mother. Even as Fricka speaks of domestic bliss, Wotan's thoughts still remain fixed on descending to Erda.

The following is the last tremolo scoring used in <u>Das Rheingold.</u> It expresses the dualism between the dreamlike palace, and Wotan's care and worry.

Trem Ex 34: iv, 913. Wotan: AThe night is nigh from all its ills. (Valhalla) offers shelter now. B(As though seized by a great thought, very firmly) CSo hail to our home! Safe from dismay and dread!D

The tremolo violin-viola-cello combination sounds At Point A as Wotan speaks of the surreal beauty of Valhalla which insulates him from suffering. At Point B, the full string tremolo indicates a great inspiration in Wotan's thoughts. The tremolo violin and viola at Point C represent Wotan's advice to the gods to accept Valhalla as their home. The full string tremolo at Point D serves to reinforce the previous scoring at Point B, as Wotan now asks Fricka to join him in Valhalla.

Wagner uses the string tremolo to add to the rising emotional disturbance we find in these scenes. It is another vehicle for him to express extra-musical ideas through orchestral color.

ANALYSES OF INSTRUMENTAL SECTIONS

Das Rheingold includes four instrumental sections, and it is here that Wagner utilizes programmatic scoring to express ideas not explicitly stated in the libretto. This helps him to fill gaps in the story in the much the same way that a comic book artist implies the ideas that transpire "between the panels."

In the following three analyses[37], I assign symbols to scorings that recur frequently within the opera. These scorings have evidenced an association with a particular extra-musical concept by means of their accumulation throughout Das Rheingold. The horn, for instance, aligns itself with ideas of light, fairness, and godliness numerous times. Likewise, the clarinet-bass clarinet combination often suggests the Nibelungs. The symbols "add up" to imply actions, encounters between characters, and commentary beyond motivic statements. Interpretation of motivic statement scoring links the meaning of the motive with the general scoring symbolism.

Although the analyses note all possible symbolic associations, it is unlikely that Wagner meant to imbue every single scoring with programmatic intention. Some are purely coloristic in nature. The large amount of evidence linking many recurring scorings with literary concepts, however, suggests that Wagner meant to imply extra-musical ideas that would enable listeners to unify some elements in the story. Utilizing orchestral color in this way, Wagner is able to present a smooth, continuous storyline that parallels his unbroken river of music.

I have formatted the analyses in the following manner: a list of the motives that appear in the section, followed by a table that examines the chronological progression of the scorings separated into motives and other figures. Following this, there is a grouped summary list that shows how scoring groups correspond to symbolic meanings. Finally, I offer an interpretation that weaves both leitmotives and scoring symbols into a narrative.

---

[37] I do not present an analysis of the first twenty bars of scene two, as this section has been covered in the article on the Valhalla motive.

ANALYSIS OF SCORINGS VS. SYMBOLIC MEANINGS—PRELUDE

Here are the motives that appear in the prelude:

Nature motive

Rhine River motive A

Rhine River motive B (ripples)--can appear in eighth notes

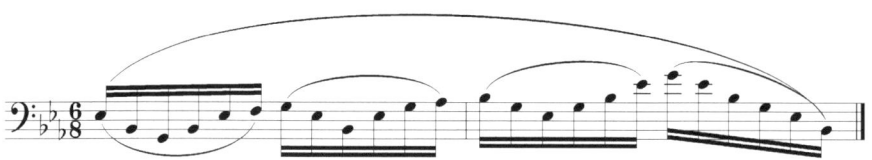

TABLE VI: PRELUDE SCORINGS

BAR	SUSTAIN (spark of creation)	NATURE MOTIVE	THE RHINE MOTIVE A	THE RHINE MOTIVE A (rhythmic counter-theme)	THE RHINE MOTIVE B (Ripples)	ASCENDING SCALE
1-4	Cb (Darkness)					
5-16	Cb, Fag (Darkness)					
17-44	Cb, Fag (Darkness)	Hn (Light)				
45-46	Cb, Fag, BCl, CBT (Darkness)	Hn (Light)				
47-48	Cb, BCl, Pos, CBT (Darkness)	Hn (Light)[38]				
49-54	Cb, Fag, Pos, CBT (Darkness)	Hn (Light)	Fag (Gloom)		Vc (Hidden depths)	
55-56	Cb, BCl, Pos, CBT (Darkness)	Hn (Light)	Fl, Fag (Lightness, gloom)		Vc (Hidden depths)	
57-60	Cb, BCl, Pos, CBT (Darkness)	Hn (Light)	Fl, Fag (Lightness, gloom)		Br, Vc (Coveting)	

[38] Dissolves into overlapping arpeggios.

BAR	SUSTAIN (spark of creation)	NATURE MOTIVE	THE RHINE MOTIVE A	THE RHINE MOTIVE A (rhythmic counter-theme)	THE RHINE MOTIVE B (Ripples)	ASCENDING SCALE
61-64	Cb, BCl, Pos, CBT (Darkness)	Hn (Light)	Fl, Fag (Lightness, gloom)		Vn, Br (Warning)	
65-76	Cb, BCl, Pos, CBT (Darkness)	Hn (Light)	Fl, Fag (Lightness, gloom)[39]		Vn (Innocence)	
77-80	Cb, BCl, Pos, CBT (Darkness)	Hn (Light)	Fl, Fag (Lightness, gloom)		Vn, Br (Warning)	
81-96	Cb, Pos, CBP, CBT (Darkness)	Hn (Light)	Fl, Fag (lightness, gloom)	Cl, BCl (Hate; Nibelung scorn)	Vc (Hidden depths)	
97-112	Cb, Pos, CBP, CBT (Darkness)	Hn (Light)	Fl, Fag (lightness, gloom)	Hb, Eng, Hn, Cl, BCl (Nibelung power)	Vn, Br, Vc (Toil)	

---

[39] Dissolves into fragment.

BAR	SUSTAIN (spark of creation)	NATURE MOTIVE	THE RHINE MOTIVE A	THE RHINE MOTIVE A (rhythmic counter-theme)	THE RHINE MOTIVE B (Ripples)	ASCENDING SCALE
113-116	Cb, Pos, CBP, CBT (Darkness)	Hn (Light)	Fag, Tr, BTr (Gloom, celebration, dormancy)	Fl, Hb,Eng. Hn, Cl, BCl, Fag (Nibelung power)	Vn, Br, Vc (Toil)	
117-128	Cb, Pos, CBP, CBT (Darkness)	Hn (Light)	Fl, Fag, Tr, Btr (Gloom, lightness, celebration, dormancy)	Fl, Hb,Eng. Hn, Cl, BCl, Fag (Nibelung power)	Vn, Br, Vc (Toil)	
129-136	Cb, Pos, CBP, CBT (Darkness)	Hn (Light)	Fl, Fag, Tr, Btr (Gloom, lightness, celebration, dormancy)	Fl, Hb, Eng. Hn, Cl, BCl, Fag (Nibelung power)	Vn, Br, Vc (Toil)	Vc, Cl, BCl, Fag/ Vn, Fl, Hb, Eng.Hn, Cl, BCl, Fag/ Vc, Eng.Hn, Cl, BCl, Fag (Secrecy, hate, Nibelung power)

SUMMARY OF SCORINGS USED IN PRELUDE

Creation Sustain

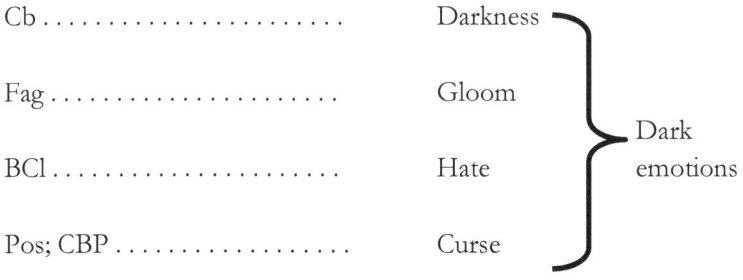

Cb . . . .   Darkness

Fag . . . .   Gloom

BCl . . . .   Hate   Dark emotions

Pos; CBP . . . .   Curse

Nature motive

Hn . . . .   Light

The Rhine motive A

Fag . . . .   Gloom

Fl, Fag . . . .   Lightness; gloom

Fl, Fag, Tr, BTr . . . .   Lightness; gloom; celebration; dormancy   Contrasts

The Rhine motive A (rhythmic counter-theme)

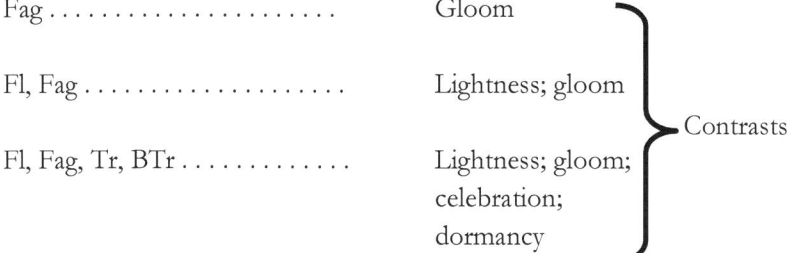

Cl, BCl . . . .   Nibelung scorn

(Fl), Hb, Eng. Hn, Cl, BCl, Fag . .   Nibelung power   Negativity

The Rhine motive B (ripples)

Vn	Innocence
Vn, Br	Warning
Br, Vc	Coveting
Vc	Hidden Depths
Vn, Br, Vc	Toil

Emotional states

Ascending scales

Vc, Cl, BCl, Fag/
Vn, Fl, Hb, Eng.Hn, Cl, BCl, Fag/ Vc,
Eng.Hn, Cl, BCl, Fag Hn, Cl, BCl, Fag

Secrecy; hate;
Nibelung power

PRELUDE ANALYSIS

In the prelude to <u>Das Rheingold</u>, Wagner portrays the beginning of the world's elements. He also begins to establish associations between orchestral timbres and programmatic references that will continue to develop and accumulate throughout the work. Here is an analysis that interprets the prelude in terms of symbols depicted by orchestral timbres.

Wagner's first scorings build a foundation that parallels the plot elements of <u>Das Rheingold</u> in terms of its contrasts. The compositional process of the prelude is one of continuous growth that begins with a sustained low Eb in the double bass which continues for the duration of the prelude. This low Eb represents the spark of creation. During the course of the prelude, Wagner amplifies this sustained tone with bassoon, bass clarinet, trombone, contrabass trombone, contrabass trombone, and contrabass tuba. In the course of the opera, these instruments will come to represent gloom, hate, curse, and agony, but in the prelude, they join with the double bass to represent the forces of darkness as personified by the Nibelung race. In contrast to this, a canon for eight horns appears, representing the forces of light. Wagner will refine this reference to light later in the opera by associating it with the gods of Valhalla, justice, and Freia.

Next, we hear two complementing themes played simultaneously by the bassoon which will come to represent gloom, and cello, which will indicate hidden depths. The bassoon theme is later developed into somewhat of a contrast as the flute, representing lightness, joins the bassoon's reference to gloom. Added later to this theme are the trumpet and bass trumpet, themselves a contrast in that one will later represent celebration and the other will signify dormancy. Later in the opera, the combination of the two will represent victory.

The cello theme continues through many different string permutations, each of which will come to symbolize a different emotional state of being. A third accompanying theme enters in the clarinet and bass clarinet (later accompanied by flute, oboe, English horn, and bassoon), representing the negative emotions of scorn and distaste which will eventually emerge as symbols for Nibelung power.

As the prelude draws to a close, the scale, used in scene three to represent Alberich's defiance, is played by the instruments representing Alberich's power. The general outlay of the prelude thus becomes a contrast in the largest sense as the horns in the opening represent the forces of Valhalla, and the woodwind combinations at the end represent the Nibelungs' power and defiance which will eventually end the Ring.

Again, I caution: Although the preceding analysis accounts for a symbolic association with every instrument, I don't believe that Wagner meant to imbue every single scoring in this prelude with programmatic intention. The rising strings could simply express orchestral color as the river forms. From a purely sonorous point of view, the flute could simply be highlighting the bassoon figure. This is Wagner's world, however, and no composer of his era utilized orchestral instruments as equal partners of the human actors to the degree that he did. Even disregarding some scorings as purely coloristic, the orchestral symbolism of the prelude suggests a natural world which is flawed almost from the moment of creation; a dynamic struggle between the gods and the Nibelungs.

HORN CANON ANALYSIS: PRELUDE

One of the most outstanding anomalies in the orchestration of Das Rheingold is the set of eight horns used in the prelude.[40] The immediate question that comes to mind is: Why eight horns? Why not seven or nine horns? The answer is that Wagner was interested in expressing the origins of music, as well as satisfying all permutations of the Eb major chord which forms the prelude. The first interval used in the prelude is the octave found between the first and second double basses. The bassoon enters at the fifth. It seems from this that Wagner intended to imitate the overtone series as a symbol of natural purity. In his horn canon, the first time two horns play together, they begin at the interval of a fifth. On the entrance of the third horn, we hear the interval of a major third. When the fourth horn enters, the interval of a minor third is heard, forming the first four intervals of the overtone series. It also provides a full major triad with a doubled

---

[40] Likewise, the six harps found at the end of Das Rheingold allow Wagner to sound all three degrees of the Db major chord both ascending and descending.

root. Thus, the first half of the <u>Rheingold</u> horn canon forms with entrances one bar apart, occurring on the first beat of the bar.

The fifth horn enters when the other four horns again achieve the doubled root triad. The sixth horn forms an octave with the fifth horn upon its entrance. Wagner again imitates the overtone series by introducing the intervals of the perfect fifth and perfect fourth when the seventh horn enters. Upon the entrance of the eighth horn, Wagner establishes two equal canons of four horns each, each containing a triad with a doubled root. Any more, any fewer than eight fails to meet these properties of symmetry, balance, and harmonic doubling.

ANALYSIS OF SCORINGS VS. SYMBOLIC MEANINGS—FIRST INTERLUDE

These motives appear in the first interlude:

Greeting to Rheingold motive (note accompaniment)

Renunciation of Love motive

Sorrow motive

The Ring motive

TABLE VII: FIRST INTERLUDE SCORINGS

BAR	MOTIVE	SCORING	SYMBOL	ACCOMPANIMENT	SYMBOL
1-2				Fag, BCl Sustain Vc moving sustain	Hate Solitude
3-6	Greeting accompaniment	Vc	Solitude	Hn, BCl, CBT, Pauk sustain; (Cb pizz.)	Resentment, Agony, Force
7-10	Greeting accompaniment	Br,Vc/Vn, Br/Vn	Loge/Advice/ Rheinmaidens (innocence)	Hb, Eng. Hn, Cl, TBTbs, Pauk sustain; (Cb pizz.)	Beauty, Agony, Force
11-12	Greeting accompaniment	Vn,[Br,Vc]	Rheinmaidens, (Loge)	Hb, Eng. Hn, Cl, Hn, Fag, Pauk sustain; Cb pizz.	Nibelung Frustration, Force
13-18	Greeting accompaniment	Vn,[Br,Vc]	Rheinmaidens, (Loge)	Fl, Hb, Eng. Hn, Cl, Hn, Fag, Pauk sustain; (Cb)	Lightness, Nibelung Frustration, Force
19-24	Greeting accompaniment	Vn,[Br,Vc]/ Vc/ Vn, Br, [Vc]/ Br,Vc	Rheinmaidens, (Loge)/ Solitude/ Advice,(Solitude)/ Loge	Hb, Eng. Hn, Hn, Fag, Tbs, Pauk sustain; (Cb)	World rule for ring, Agony, Force

BAR	MOTIVE	SCORING	SYMBOL	ACCOMPANIMENT	SYMBOL
25-26	Greeting accompaniment	Vc	Solitude	Eng. Hn, TBTbs, Pauk sustain	Helplessness, Agony, Force
27-28	Greeting accompaniment	Vc	Solitude	Eng.Hn,Cl,BCl,Pauk sustain (Cb) pizz.	Hate, Force
29-30	Greeting accompaniment	Vc	Solitude	Eng.Hn,Cl,BCl,Hn,Pauk sustain	Resentment, Force
31-33	Greeting accompaniment; Renunciation	Vc; Eng. Hn, Hn (Pauk) (BCl, Pauk)	Solitude; despair (resentment)	Tbs sustain. Cb pizz.	Agony
34	Renunciation; Sorrow	Hb, Eng.Hn, Hn (Pauk); Tbs	Stealing gold; Agony	Trem. Vn, Br sustain; Pauk, Tr attacks Cb, Trem. Vc chromatic	Agitation, warning, heartbeat Darkness, insanity, isolation
35				Hb, Eng. Hn transition figure Cl chromatic Trem. Vn, Br sustain Pauk, Tr attacks Cb, trem. Vc chromatic	Stealing gold Nibelung Agitation, Warning, Heartbeat Darkness, insanity, isolation

BAR	MOTIVE	SCORING	SYMBOL	ACCOMPANIMENT	SYMBOL
36-37	Ring	(Hb), Eng. Hn, Cl	Beauty	Cb, Trem Vc, BCl sustain (Tr, Pauk, Cym attack)	Darkness, insanity, isolation, hate; Heartbeat
38-39	Greeting accompaniment	Vn	Rheinmaidens	Fl arpeggio; Trem Vc, (Cl), BCl sustain	Lightness; Insanity, isolation, hate
40-41	Ring	Fag	Gloom	Hn, Pauk sustain; (Cb)	Valhalla, Force
42-43	Greeting accompaniment	Fl	Lightness	Vn arpeggio; Hn, Fag, Pauk sustain	Tenderness; Payment, Force
44-45	Ring	Br	Denial	Hn, Pauk sustain; (Vc, Cb pizz.)	Gods of Valhalla, Force
46-47	Greeting accompaniment	Harp	Twinkling Beauty	Fl arpeggio; Hn, Br, Pauk sustain	Lightness; Distrust, Force
48-51	Ring	Hn	Gods of Valhalla	Vc, Cb sustain	Darkness
52-56	Ring	Hn	Gods of Valhalla	Vc sustain	Privacy

SUMMARY OF SCORINGS USED IN FIRST INTERLUDE

Motivic Statements

Sorrow motive

Tbs . . . .   Agony

Greeting to Rheingold motive (accompaniment)

Vn . . . .   Rheinmaidens
(innocence)

Vn, Br . . . .   Advice*

Br, Vc . . . .   Loge*

Vc . . . .   Privacy, Isolation

The Ring motive

(Hb), Eng. Hn, Cl . . . .   Beauty*

Br . . . .   Denial

Fag . . . .   Gloom

Hn . . . .   Valhalla

Renunciation of Love motive

Eng. Hn, Hn . . . .   Despair*

Eng. Hn, BCl, Hn . . . .   Resentment*

* Unique scoring of this motive. Symbolic meaning inferred from similar recurring scorings of other motives or from combinations used sparingly in the first scene.

SUMMARY OF SCORINGS USED IN FIRST INTERLUDE (cont'd)

Non-motivic material[41]

Vc.	Solitude
Vc, Cb	Darkness
Hn, Br	Distrust
Fag, BCl	Hate
Tbs	Agony
Hb, Eng. Hn, Cl	Beauty
(Fl), Hb, Eng. Hn, Cl, Hn, Fag . . .	Nibelung frustration
Hn, BCl, CBT; . . . . Eng. Hn, Cl, BCl, Hn; Eng. Hn, BCl, Hn	Resentment
Fl	Lightness
Vn	Tenderness
Eng. Hn, Cl, BCl	Distaste
Eng. Hn	Helplessness
Hb, Eng. Hn, Hn, Fag	World rule for ring
Hb, Eng. Hn; . . . . Hb, Eng. Hn, Hn	Stealing gold

---

[41] Symbolic content of non-motivic material is inferred by symbolic role of similar combinations found in motivic statements.

FIRST INTERLUDE ANALYSIS

The first interlude begins after Alberich steals the gold when Wagner tells us that Alberich's laughter is heard in the distance, then the rocks begin to disappear in the darkness. It ends at the beginning of the second scene, 56 bars later.

An analysis of orchestral symbolism divides this interlude into two sections: the Rheinmaidens talking to Loge, and four portraits of the ring. Most of the scorings used in this interlude have been used very sparingly up to this point in the opera, and many refer to specific lines in the text.

1-35. In bars 1-6, we first hear the cello-bassoon-bass clarinet combination holding a chord representing hate and privacy. The bass clarinet fades into the background as the cello becomes more prominent. It plays the rippling figure that accompanied the Greeting to the Rheingold motive. Since the non-motivic accompaniment also bears symbols for resentment and agony, we see a dualism emerging between the cello, which represents a calm privacy, and the angry, resentful chord behind it. The interpretation of the first six bars thus includes two characters; one, the Nibelung, rushing away from the Rheinmaidens, hurt by their taunting, and the other, a lone, hidden figure making his way through the waves.

In bars 7-10, the chordal accompaniment remains constant, containing symbols of beauty and agony. The motivic accompaniment figure changes scoring from viola-cello to violin-viola to violin. The violin represents the Rheinmaidens themselves singing to the gold in many statements of the Greeting to the Rheingold motive. The violin-viola statement is a unique scoring of this motive, but is used in statements of other motives to refer to advice or warning. The viola-cello combination is also a unique scoring of this motive. In bars 11-21 it exchanges figures with the violin, suggesting a dialogue between the Rheinmaidens and the character who has just entered. Later in the opera, Wagner frequently uses the viola-cello combination to refer specifically to Loge. I therefore link the viola-cello/violin exchange with a dialogue between Loge and the Rheinmaidens. The analysis of bars

7-10 reveals the Rheinmaidens singing to Loge (who has embarked on the journey mentioned in his scene two narrative) and asking his advice.

The violin vs. viola-cello scoring of the figure in bars 11-21 represents an exchange between Loge and the Rheinmaidens. The sustaining chords contain symbols of Nibelung frustration replaced by a scoring representing world rule for the owner of the ring. This suggests that the Rheinmaidens reveal to Loge that they frustrated the Nibelung, who then overheard them discussing the power of the ring.

In bars 22-30, the sustained accompaniment changes from a symbol of world rule for the ring coupled with agony, to an indication of helplessness, and finally to distaste and resentment. In this section, the Rheinmaidens tell Loge of their helplessness as Alberich found the gold preferable to his fruitless pursuit of love. His distaste for the Rheinmaidens grew into the resentment which would cause him to renounce love.

In bars 31-33, the English horn and horn play the Renunciation motive with the tubas sustaining. The English horn-horn combination is a rare scoring that seems to represent despair. The tubas represent agony. Wagner adds the bass clarinet to the scoring of the Renunciation motive to indicate resentment. The scorings refer to Alberich's despair giving way to the resentment which caused him to steal the gold.

Bars 34-35 are transitional figures that encapsulate the story of the robbery of the Rheingold. The oboe, English horn, and horn play the Renunciation motive to represent Alberich's robbery. The tubas play the Sorrow motive, representing agony. The accompaniment contains an onomatopoetic reference to a heartbeat, as well as symbols of mental uneasiness, darkness, isolation, and warning. The programmatic scoring in this very brief section allows Wagner to describe Alberich's warning as he sprang up to the gold to steal it, his heart pounding, and disappeared into the darkness.

Bars 36-56. In bars 36-56, we segue from the immediate vicinity of the Rhine to four portraits of the nature of the ring. The first uses the English horn and clarinet to represent its beauty. Underlying the ring's beauty, however, are symbols of the dark, frenzied isolation and hate that result from the curse of love necessary to wield its power.

The scene changes upward in bars 38-39, and we hear a fainter indication of the Rheinmaidens' cries coupled with the new lightness that begins to emerge.

In bars 40-41, we hear the second portrait of the ring, now played by the bassoon underscored by the horn. This represents the gloomy fate of the ring as the gods will use it. Bars 42-43 indicate the change of scene upward to the third picture of the ring, played in bars 44-45 by the viola underlined by the horn, representing the gods' eventual forfeiture of the ring.

In bars 46-47, the last shimmer of the Rhine disappears from view as the new light of Valhalla becomes more apparent. We hear a note of distrust (Hn-Br) as we move toward the final picture of the ring in bars 48-56, played by the horn underlined by the lower strings. This final portrait shows the ring as the prize of Valhalla, noble, yet surrounded by an eerie darkness.

ANALYSIS OF SCORINGS VS. SYMBOLIC MEANINGS— SECOND AND THIRD INTERLUDES

These motives appear in the second and third interludes:

Loge

Woman's worth

Sorrow

We - he!   ach   we - he!

Flight (note section marked A)

Rheingold

Smiths

Love/Resignation (see section marked A)

The Ring motive

Renunciation of Love motive

Nur wer der Min - ne Macht ver - sagt,

Arrogance of Power

TABLE VIII: SECOND INTERLUDE SCORINGS

BAR	MOTIVE	SCORING	SYMBOL	ACCOMPANIMENT	SYMBOL
1-4	Loge	Br, Vc	Loge's character	(Cb, Fag chromatic)	(Darkness, Gloom)
5-7	Loge	Vn, Br, Vc	Toil	(Cb, Fag chromatic)	(Darkness, Gloom)
8-9	Loge	Vn, Br, Vc	Toil	(Fl) Eng.Hn, Fag chromatic down; Fag,BCl,BTb,Cb chromatic up	Withering; Hate, Agony, Darkness
10-11	Loge	Vn, Br, Vc/ Vn, Br	Toil/ Advice	Fl, Eng.Hn, Cl, Fag chromatic down; Fag,BCl,BTb,Cb chromatic up	Nibelung rule; Hate, Agony, Darkness
12	Loge	Vn, Br, Vc, Eng. Hn, Cl, Fag	Toil, Nibelung rule	BCl, BTb, Cb tritones	Onomatopoetic representation of plodding
13	Loge	Br, Vc, Fag	Doom for the gods	CBT, Cb tritones	Plodding
14-15	Woman's worth	Pos	Curse	CBT, BTb, CBP sustain; Cb pizz.	Agony, Curse
16-17	Loge	Vc	Privacy	BCl Fag sustain; Cb pizz.	Hate

BAR	MOTIVE	SCORING	SYMBOL	ACCOMPANIMENT	SYMBOL
18-19	Woman's worth	Pos	Curse	CBT, BTb, CBP sustain. Cb pizz.	Agony, Curse
20-21	Loge	Br, Vc	Loge's character	Pos, CBP sustain; Cb pizz.	Curse
22-23	Woman's worth	Hn	Freia	Hn, Cb sustain	Fairness, Darkness
24	Loge	Vn, Br, Vc	Toil (foreshadows harmonic structure)	Hn, BTb, CBT sustain	Fairness, Agony
25	Loge	Vn, Br, Vc	Toil	BtB, CBT sustain	Agony
26-27	Woman's worth	Hn	Freia	Hn, Cb sustain	Fairness, Darkness
28-29	Sorrow	Vc/Hb, Eng. Hn, Cl	Privacy/Beauty	Hn, BTb, CBT, Pauk sustain	Fairness, Agony, Force
30-31	Sorrow	Vc/Fl, Hb, Eng. Hn., Cl, BCl, Fag	Privacy/Dislike	Hn, BTb, CBT, Pauk sustain	Fairness, Agony, Force
32-33	Flight	Vc (Hn)	Privacy (Freia)	Fag, BTb, CBT, Pauk sustain. Cb pizz.	Gloom, Agony, Force
34-35	Flight	Br, Vc (Hn)	Coveting (Freia)	Fag, BTb, CBT, Pauk sustain. Cb pizz.	Gloom, Agony, Force
36-38	Flight	Vn, Br, Vc (Hn)	Toil (Freia)	Fag, BTb, CBT, Pauk sustain. Cb pizz.	Gloom, Agony, Force

BAR	MOTIVE	SCORING	SYMBOL	ACCOMPANIMENT	SYMBOL
39–43	Flight	Vn, Br, Vc (Hb, Hn, Cl)	Toil (Nibelung aspirations)	Fag, BTb, CBT, Pauk sustain. Cb pizz.	Gloom, Agony, Force
44–45	Flight Rheingold (minor)	Vn, Br, Vc BTr	Toil Dormancy	Hb, Fag, Hn, Cl, BTb, CBT, Pauk sustain. Cb arco.	Nibelung aspirations, Agony, Force
46–49	Ring	Vn, Br, Vc	Toil	Hb, Fag, Hn, Cl, BTb, CBT, Pauk sustain. Cb arco.	Nibelung aspirations, Agony, Force
50–56	Smiths Rheingold (minor) → Love/Resignation	Vn, Br, Vc,Hb, Fag, Hn, Cl Tr, BTr	Toil, Nibelung aspirations Victory	Pos, CBP, BTb, CBT, Pauk sustain with Rheingold motive.	Curse, Agony, Force
57–58	Smiths Love/Resignation	Vn, Br, Vc, Hn Tr, BTr	Toil, Fairness Victory	Hb, Cl, Fag, Pos, CBP, BTb, CBT, Pauk sustain	Nibelung aspirations, Curse, Agony, Force
59–63	Smiths Love/Resignation	Anvils, Vn, Br, Vc, Hn Pos	Smiths, Toil, Fairness. Curse	Pauk sustain Cb pizz.	Force

BAR	MOTIVE	SCORING	SYMBOL	ACCOMPANIMENT	SYMBOL
64	Smiths	Anvils, Vn, Br, Vc	Smiths, Toil	Pauk sustain	Force
	Love/ Resignation	Pos	Curse		
65-66	Smiths	Anvils, Vn, Br	Smiths, Dare	Pauk sustain	Force
	Love/ Resignation	Pos	Curse		
67-74	Smiths	Anvils	Smiths		
75-82	Smiths	Anvils, Vn, Br	Smiths, Dare		
	Love/ Resignation	Vc, Cb, Fag	Darkness, Gloom		
83-85	Smiths	Anvils, Vn, Br	Smiths, Dare		
	Sorrow	Vc, Cb, Fag	Nibelheim		
86	Smiths	(Anvils), Vn, Br, Vc	(Smiths), Toil	Hn, Fag, Cb sustain	Valhalla, Gloom, Darkness
87-89	Ring (varied)	Vn, Br, Vc	Toil	Fl, Hb, Cl, Hn, (Fag) sustain	Nibelung aspirations
90	Ring (varied)	Br, Vc/Vc, Cb	Coveting/ Darkness		

BAR	MOTIVE	SCORING	SYMBOL	ACCOMPANIMENT	SYMBOL
iii, 112-114				Trem Vn, Br, Vc chromatic up	Toil, Agitation
				Fl, Hb, Fag, Pauk, Tr, Btr sustain. (Cb attack)	Nibelung aspirations, Force, Victory
iii, 115-117	Smiths	St. Hn, Pauk	Insult, Force	Vn, Br, Vc (Cb) attacks	Toil
				Pos, CBP mimic Alberich's laugh	Curse
				Klf, Hb, Cl, Fag trill	Mocking, Nibelung aspirations
iii, 118-120	Smiths	Vn, Br	Dare	Hb, Fag, St. Hn, Cl, Fl, Klf, Pauk attack	Mocking, Nibelung aspirations, Force
	Sorrow	BTb, CBT, Vc, Cb	Agony, Darkness		
iii, 121-126	Smiths	Vn, Br	Dare	Hb, Fag, St. Hn, Cl attack. Pauk punctuate.	Nibelung aspirations, Force
	Sorrow	BTb, CBT, Vc, Cb	Agony, Darkness		
iii, 127-132	Smiths	Vc, Cb	Darkness	St. Hn, Pauk attack	Insult, Force
	Sorrow	Hb, Cl, Pos/Vn, Br	Nibelung tragedy, Curse/Warning		

BAR	MOTIVE	SCORING	SYMBOL	ACCOMPANIMENT	SYMBOL
iii, 133-135	Smiths	Fag, Cb	Gloom, Darkness	Vn, Br pizz.	
	Sorrow	Pos, CBP/ Hb, Cl	Curse/ Nibelung tragedy		
iii, 136	Loge	Br, Vc	Loge's character	Pos, CBP, BTb, CBT, Pauk sustain	Curse, Agony, Force

TABLE IX: THIRD INTERLUDE SCORINGS

BAR	MOTIVE	SCORING	SYMBOL	ACCOMPANIMENT	SYMBOL
1-2	Arrogance	(Fl) Hb, Fag, Hn, Cl	Nibelung aspirations	Vn, Br, Pauk trill	Threat, Force
3	Arrogance	Vn, Br, (Fl, Hb, Fag, Hn, Cl)	Threat (Nibelung aspirations)	Fl, Hb, Cl, Pauk trill Hn, Fag sustain	Nibelung tragedy, Force, Payment
4-5	Loge	Vn, Br, (Vc, (Fl) Hb, Fag, Hn, Cl)	Advice (Privacy, Nibelung aspirations)	KlF, Fl,Hb, Cl, Pauk trill Hn, Fag sustain	Nibelung tragedy, Force, Mocking, Payment
6-7	Arrogance	KlF, Fl, Vn, Br, (Fl, Hb, Fag, Hn, Cl)	Mocking, Threat (Nibelung aspirations)	Pauk, Vc, (triangle) trill Hn, Fag sustain	Force, Privacy, Mirth, Payment
8-17	Ring	Vn, Br	Warning	(Fl) Hb, Fag, Hn, Cl, Pauk, Vc, Cb sustain	Nibelung aspirations, Force, Darkness
18-20	Ring	Vn, Br	Warning	Cl, Fag, Vc, Cb, Pauk sustain	Nibelung, Darkness, Force
21-22	Woman's Worth	Pos (Eng, Hn, Fag)	Curse (Withering)	Pauk, Vc, Cb sustain	Force, Darkness
23-30	Smiths	Br, (Vc)	Denial (Craving)	Pauk sustain (Cb pizz.)	Force
	Sorrow	BTb, CBT	Agony		

BAR	MOTIVE	SCORING	SYMBOL	ACCOMPANIMENT	SYMBOL
31-38	Smiths	Anvil	Smiths	(Cb pizz.)	
39-46	Smiths	Anvil	Smiths	Tbs, Pauk sustain	Agony, Force
	Love/Resignation	Horn	Freia		
47-50				Pos, CBP sustain	Curse
51-52	Giants	Vc, Cb	Craving		
53	Giants	Vc, Cb	Craving		
	Arrogance	Fag	Gloom		
54	Giants	Vc, Cb	Craving		
	Arrogance	Hn, Fag	Payment		
55	Loge	Vc	Privacy	Fl, Hb, Fag, BTb, CBT sustain	Nibelung aspiration, Agony
56	Loge	Br, Vc	Loge's character	Fl, Hb, Fag, Hn, BTb, CBT sustain	Nibelung aspiration, Agony

BAR	MOTIVE	SCORING	SYMBOL	ACCOMPANIMENT	SYMBOL
57-58	Loge	Vn	Tenderness	Fl, Hb, Fag, Hn, BTb, CBT sustain. (Vc, Cb attack)	Nibelung aspiration, Agony
59-60	Giants	Vc, Cb (Br pizz)	Craving (Tenderness)		
61	Giants	Vc, Cb (Br pizz)	Craving (Tenderness)		
	Arrogance	Hn, Fag	Payment		
62	Giants	Vc, Cb (Br pizz)	Craving (Tenderness)		
	Arrogance	Hn, Fag, Cl	Nibelung aspiration		
63-64	Loge	(Br)Vc	Privacy (Loge's character)	KlF, Fl, Hb, Fag, Hn, Cl, BTb, CBT sustain	Mocking, Nibelung aspirations, Agony
65-66	Loge	Vn	Tenderness	KlF, Fl, Hb, Fag, Hn, Cl, BTb, CBT sustain (Vc, Cb attack)	Mocking, Nibelung aspirations, Agony
67-68	Giants (var.)	Vc, Cb (TTb)	Craving (Agony)		
69-70	Giants	Hn, Fag (TTb) (Vc, Cb)	Payment (Agony) (Craving)		

BAR	MOTIVE	SCORING	SYMBOL	ACCOMPANIMENT	SYMBOL
71-74	Giants (var.)	Hn, Fag, Br, Vc, Cb (Pos)	Payment, Toil (Curse)		
75-76	Loge	Br, Vc (Vn, Cl, BCl, Fag)	Loge's character	Pos, BTb, CBT sustain	Curse, Agony
77-80	Arrogance	Br	Denial	(Hb), Eng, Hn, Cl sustain (foreshadows Renunciation)	Beauty
81-82	Loge	Vn	Tenderness	BCl, Pauk sustain (Vc, Cb pizz.)	Hate, Force
	Renunciation (fragment)	Hn	Freia		
83-84	Loge	Vn, Br	Warning	BCl, Pauk sustain (Vc, Cb pizz.)	Hate, Force
	Renunciation (fragment)	Hn, Fag	Payment		
85	Loge	Vn, Br	Warning	BCl, Pauk, Cb, BTb sustain	Hate, Force, Darkness, Agony
	Renunciation (fragment)	Fl, Hn, Fag, Cl	Nibelung aspiration		

102

BAR	MOTIVE	SCORING	SYMBOL	ACCOMPANIMENT	SYMBOL
86	Loge	Vn, Br, Vc	Toil	BCl, Pauk, Cb, BTb sustain	Hate, Force, Darkness, Agony
	Renunciation (fragment)	Fl, Hn, Fag, Cl	Nibelung aspiration		
87-88	Renunciation	(KlF) Fl, Hb, Fag, Hn, Cl, trem. Str.	(Mocking), Nibelung aspiration, Anger, Agitation	BCl, Pauk, (Pos),BTb, Pauk sustain	Hate, Force, Agony, (Curse)
89-90	Greeting to Gold/Sorrow	Fl, Hb, Eng, Hn, Cl, Fag/ Vn, Br, Vc	Nibelung rule/Toil	Hn, Pauk, sustain. Cb pizz.	Fairness, Force
91-94	Sorrow	Vn, Br, Vc	Toil	Hn, Fag, Pauk, sustain. (Cb pizz.)	Payment, Force
95-96	Loge	KlF, Fl, Hb, Cl	Mocking, Nibelung tragedy	Hn, Fag, Pauk, CBT sustain. Str. Attack	Payment, Agony, Force, Anger
97-98	Loge	Vn	Tenderness	Hn, Fag, CBT, Pauk sustain	Payment, Agony, Force
99-100	Loge	Fag, Br, Vc	Doom for the gods	BCl, Hn, Fag, CBT, Pauk sustain	Hate, Payment, Agony, Force
101-104	Loge	BCl, Fag, Br, Vc	Hate, Loge's character		
105-112	Sorrow	Strings	Anger	Hn, Str attack	Valhalla, Anger

SUMMARY OF SCORINGS USED IN SECOND AND THIRD INTERLUDES

Motivic Statements

Sorrow motive

Vn, Br . . . . . .   Enslavement

Vc . . . .   Privacy

Vc, Cb . . . . . .   Darkness

Vn, Br, Vc . .   Labor

Str. . . . .   Anger

Vc, Cb, Fag . .   Opening to Nibelheim

Fl, Hb, Eng. Hn, ... Cl, BCl, Fag   Hate

Hb, Eng. Hn, Cl . . . . . .   Beauty

Hb, Cl . . . . . .   Nibelung tragedy*

Fl, Hb, Eng. Hn, ... Cl, Fag   Nibelung Rule*

Pos, CBP . . .   Curse

BTb, CBT . . .   Agony

Rheingold motive

Btr . . . .   Dormancy; Passivity

Tr, BTr . . . . .   Victory

Greeting to Rheingold motive

Vn, Br, Vc . . . .   Suffering

Fl, Hb, Eng. Hn, . . . Cl, Fag   Nibelung rule

Ring motive

Vn, Br . . . .   Warning

Br, Vc . . . .   Coveting

Vc, Cb . . . .   Darkness*

Vn, Br, Vc . . . .   Suffering; Toil

Renunciation of love motive

Hn . . . .   Freia; Gods of Valhalla; Fairness*

Hn, Fag . . . .   Payment

(Fl), Hn, Fag, Cl; . . (Fl), Hb, Hn, Fag, Cl   Nibelung aspirations to power*

KlF, Fl . . . .   Mocking*

Trem. Str. . . . .   Anger*

<u>Flight motive</u>

Vc	Privacy*
Br, Vc	Coveting*
Vn, Br, Vc	Toil*

<u>Giants motive</u>
(string symbols adjusted)

(Br)	Tenderness
Vc, Cb; (Vc, Cb) .	Craving
Br, Vc, Cb	Labor
Hn, Fag	Payment
(Pos)	Curse
TTbs	Agony

* Unique scoring of this motive. Symbolic meaning inferred from similar recurring scorings of other motives.

SUMMARY OF SCORINGS USED IN SECOND AND THIRD INTERLUDES

Motivic Statements, (cont'd)

Loge motive		Woman's worth motive	
Vn	Tenderness	(Eng. Hn, Fag) . . .	Withering; Dying*
Vn, Br	Advice		
Vc	Privacy	Hn	Freia
Br, Vc	Loge's character	Pos	Curse*
Vn, Br, Vc.	Toil	**Nibelung smiths motive**	
Trem. Vn, Br, Vc	Toil and Agitation	Br	Denial
		Vn, Br	Dare
Cb	Darkness*	Br, Vc	Craving*
Br, Vc, Fag	Doom for the gods	Vn, Br, Vc.	Toil
		Vc, Cb	Darkness
Cb, Fag	Darkness, gloom*	Fag, Cb	Darkness, gloom*
Fl, Eng. Hn, Fag. .	Withering; Dying*	Hb, Fag, Hn, Cl . .	Nibelung aspiration*
(Fl), Eng. Hn, Cl, Fag	Nibelung rule*	Hn.	Fairness
		St. Hn, Pauk	Scorn; Force
Hb, Fag, Hn, Cl . .	Nibelung aspiration*	Anvils	Smiths at work
Cl, BCl, Fag; . . . . Fag, BCl	Hate*		
BTb	Agony*		

Arrogance of power motive		Love/resignation motive	
Br	Denial	Vc, Cb, Fag . .	Darkness; gloom*
Vn, Br	Warning	Tr, BTr	Victory*
KlF, Fl	Mocking	Hn	Freia; Fairness*
Hn, Fag. . . .	Payment	Pos.	Curse*
(Fl), Hb, Fag, Hn, Cl; Hn, Fag, Cl	Nibelung aspiration*		

* Unique scoring of this motive. Symbolic meaning inferred from similar recurring scorings of other motives.

SUMMARY OF SCORINGS USED IN SECOND AND THIRD INTERLUDES

Non-motivic material[42]

Vn, Br	Warning; Advice; Threat
Vc.	Solitude; Privacy
Vn, Br, Vc	Labor; suffering; Toil
Str	Anger
Cb; Vc, Cb	Darkness
KlF, Fl	Mocking
Hb	Naïveté; Tragedy
Fag	Gloom
Hb, Hn Cl (Fl); . . . . Hb, Fag,(Fl); Hb, Cl, Fag; Hb, Fag, St. Hn; Cl; Hb, Cl; Hb, Fag, Hn, Cl (Fl); Hb, Fag, Hn, (Fl);	Nibelung aspirations to power
Hb, Eng. Hn, Cl; . . . . Eng. Hn, Cl	Beauty
BCl; BCl, Fag	Hate
Hn	Fairness; Freia; Valhalla

---

[42] Symbolic content of non-motivic material is inferred by symbolic role of similar combinations found in motivic statements.

St. Hn . . . . Insult; Scorn

Hn, Fag . . . . Payment

Tr, BTr . . . . Victory

Pos; CBP . . . . Curse

BTb; CBT; Tbs . . . . Agony

Pauk . . . . Force

SECOND AND THIRD INTERLUDE ANALYSES

The second and third interludes contain many of the same musical ideas, so I will analyze them together. The leitmotives and symbols described on the previous pages weave together to suggest the following narratives. A stage director might use these to present visuals which bridge the gaps in the action between sections.

The second interlude traces Wotan and Loge's journey to Nibelheim. It begins as the two gods depart. Wagner tells us that the vapor thickens into a black cloud. The interlude is interrupted by the exchange between Alberich and Mime at the beginning of the third scene, then continues as Alberich's scoldings retreat in the distance and the gods descend by a shaft. The interlude ends when Loge announces, "Nibelheim, here." The interlude is divided into eight sections. The last two appear in the incidental music in scene three, the continuation of gods' journey to Nibelheim.

<u>Bars 1-13.</u> This section describes Loge's thoughts as he wanders through the gloom and darkness. He thinks about the gods withering, and about the hellish agony of Nibelheim. He ponders the state of the land ruled by Alberich. As he plods through the dark mire of the Earth, his next thoughts consider the end of the godly race.

<u>Bars 14-31.</u> This vignette may be interpreted as a first-person narrative revealing Loge's thoughts as if Wagner had verbally scripted them:

> *Loge: So be it, then! Now, devotion to Freia has become cursed. I can feel it--the hate steams up from the ground. For myself, I don't need this, but Freia should be saved. I see my two alternatives: Whether I labor for good or for evil, the gods die anyway. Rescuing Freia buys them more time. It is unfair that Freia pays for Wotan's deception, but must I continue on this awful journey?*

<u>Bars 32-43.</u> We switch from Loge's thoughts to the third-person view of the gods rushing toward Nibelheim. All their desire, all their toil is directed at

saving Freia. As they venture closer, the negative aura of Nibelheim becomes more apparent.

Bars 44-58. In this section, Wagner describes the two sides of the struggle: the gods' effort to save the slumbering Rheingold, versus the Nibelung who rules through enslavement and force. He suggests that it is power, not objects at stake in this battle. So far, Alberich's forces have been winning, much to the dismay of the Rheingold which wishes to express love through its radiance once again. As we move to the next section, we see the Rheingold enslaved at the hands of the Nibelung.

Bars 59-74. The gods labor downward into a land where love is cursed. They sneak past the anvils of the Nibelung smiths on the outskirts of Nibelheim.

Bars 75-90. As Wotan and Loge turn away from the smiths, they feel the gloom and darkness that radiates from the Nibelungs' life without love. They head toward Nibelheim proper: the center of the power struggle. They feel the Nibelung's desire for power as they make their final descent into Nibelheim.

Scene Three, Bars 112-126. This last leg of the journey to Nibelheim reminds us of Loge's toil through the rock, while the aura of Alberich's speech is still in the air. His speech earns him much fear, but no respect, as signs of mocking and contempt for his power echo from his still working slaves. This emotion fades as Alberich travels farther away from the main action.

Scene Three, Bars 127-136. Subdued by the all-seeing gaze of Alberich, the slaves toil in darkness. Wotan and Loge arrive in Nibelheim.

The third interlude of <u>Das Rheingold</u> consists of essentially the same material as the second interlude, but it is longer and is divided into eleven sections.

<u>Bars 1-7.</u> As Wotan and Loge drag Alberich up from Nibelheim, we hear Alberich's angry and arrogant, albeit impotent threats to the gods. It becomes more apparent that the gods are thinking of payment as Loge now tries to keep Alberich quiet. Physically defenseless, Alberich uses sympathy for his Nibelung race and mocking the gods as his verbal weapons. As this part of the journey ends, Loge chuckles to himself about Alberich's defeat.

<u>Bars 8-23.</u> As Alberich continues to struggle within his bonds, Wagner impresses us with a warning as it pertains to the power of the ring. It becomes plainer that the warning refers to the cursed fate the gods are resigned to follow. The transition to the next vignette prepares us for our next look at the inhabitants of Nibelheim.

<u>Bars 24-30.</u> As the gods and their captive near the smiths and their anvils, they hear the cries of agony and coming from the slaves, who have been denied freedom. Loge turns his head to notice them, but soon looks away.

<u>Bars 31-50.</u> They pass directly by the smiths at work. As they leave the anvils, we are reminded of the Nibelungs' agony, and the love of Freia as the gods head upward. These images dissolve, and we are left with the evil omen of the curse.

<u>Bars 51-57.</u> This section deals with the giants' over-confidence as they eagerly await their payment. Loge continues to wrestle with Alberich, as Alberich continues to complain. Loge tries to use his logic to subdue Alberich.

<u>Bars 58-65.</u> The scene changes from Loge's battle with the Nibelung to the anxious giants who now show themselves to be as greedy as the Nibelungs. We then segue back to Loge's running battle with Alberich.

<u>Bars 66-80.</u> The giants still crave payment. Freia is still with them. She agonizes over her condition. We are now reminded of the work for which

the giants want payment, as well as a foreshadowing of the curse which will eventually taint them. As we change back to Loge's sparring match with Alberich, we see Loge's patience wearing thin. Alberich reflects back on his unhappy past as he now prepares to admit defeat.

Bars 81-88. Now satisfied that the Nibelung is ready to surrender, Loge changes his attitude. He listens with sympathy and advice to Alberich's confession of the experiences which caused him to hate and renounce all love. Alberich speaks first of the fairness of the Rheinmaidens, and how he used the gold as compensation for love. He tells of how he renounced love to gain power. Loge tires of Alberich's tale, and the Nibelung becomes enraged, but suppresses his anger.

Bars 89-94. In this vignette, Alberich once again tries to tell Loge about how the glittering Rheingold turned to misery as he worked to gain power. Loge seems not to care, as Valhalla and payment are all that are on his mind.

Bars 95-104. Loge now arouses Alberich's anger as he mocks the dwarf's sad story. He ignores Alberich's expressions of hostility as he reflects upon the totality of the journey. Alberich's hatred toward Loge now becomes plainer.

Bars 105-112. As the gods and their prisoner return to Valhalla, Alberich burns with anger and sorrow.

ANALYSIS OF TWO VOCAL EXCERPTS

To show the practicality of considering orchestral symbols while staging Das Rheingold, I have analyzed Loge's narrative from scene two, and a brief section from scene three. I have used a method similar to the previous analyses—examine leitmotive scorings associated with dramatic action or text, then infer non-motivic material from similar scorings found in motivic statements throughout Das Rheingold. In these examples, the vocal text offers a more concrete starting point for interpretation.

ANALYSIS OF LOGE'S NARRATIVE

Loge's narrative, "Immer Ist Undank Loges Lohn," is one of the most traditionally operatic and lyrical moments in Das Rheingold. It introduces Loge and spotlights his elusive, unctuous character. Wotan has called on Loge to find an alternate payment for the Giants who have built Valhalla. Loge has failed to find a suitable substitute. He covers for his failure by presenting Wotan with an even bigger problem—Alberich has stolen the Rheingold and is in the process of forging the ring which will enable him to rule the world. The vocal text first portrays Loge as the hardworking god-on-the-street reporter surveying all beings. He is, in fact, just delaying his real news—he has no solution, that Alberich stole the gold. Once he relates this to Wotan, Loge focuses attention away from his own responsibility. He tells Wotan that the Rheinmaidens are depending on the king of the gods to return the gold. Loge reminds Wotan that he is simply the messenger.

In the thematic material, Wagner first emphasizes Freia's motive, referring to the beauty and desirability of women. As a flashback to the first scene, Wagner recalls the Rheingold's motive, mostly played in minor to indicate the troubled state of the gold. We then hear snippets of the Rheinmaidens' song, the Ring motive, and the Greeting to the Gold. As Loge ends his narrative, we hear his own motive.

Here is a detailed analysis of Wagner's scoring, its symbolic subtext, and some performance suggestions that utilize the subtext to enhance the scene.

114

> ^AThankless is ever Loge's lot.   Concerned for your sake, hoping to
> help, I scouted around to the ends of the earth. In place of Freia, I
> looked, for what the giants might accept. I sought unsuccessfully,
> and in the wide world nothing's so hard to replace in the heart of
> man as ^Bwoman's joy and worth.^C (All show astonishment and
> perplexity)
>
> ^DAll living in water earth and air, many I asked, inquired wherever
> nature springs and seeds sprout ^EWhat does man hold mightier
> than Woman's joy and worth?
>
> ^FYet in the wide world they laughed at my clever question In water,
> earth, and air none would give up love and wife. (mixed motions)
>
> ^GJust one, I saw who swore off love, for sake of some ruddy gold
> gave up woman's
> favor. ^HThe Rhine's bright children clamored their plight. The
> Nibelung, Night-Alberich
> ^Itried unsuccessfully to court them. The Rheingold ^Jrobbed in
> vengeance this thief. He thinks it the worthiest good, More noble
> than woman's grace. About their gleaming toy, from the deep torn,
> echoed the maidens' wailing.
>
> ^LTo you Wotan, they pray to do justice to the robber the gold to
> the water return, and forever stay by itself.^M
>
> ^NTo speak with you, I promised the maidens, and now have I kept
> my word.

At point A, Loge is accompanied by his signature viola-cello combination. The scoring gradually gains in presence until point B when he mentions "woman's joy and worth." There, Wagner briefly adds an English horn to the horn chord signaling woman's fairness. The addition of the English horn adds a tragic and somewhat ironic aura to the otherwise noble sonority.[43] Loge might give some increasing indications, beginning here, that he is concealing the whole truth from the gods.

The cellos play a canonically imitated figure that is related to Freia's motive. The subtext here could possibly reference Fasolt, the love-struck giant, as cello statements of Freia's motive tend to refer to his private desire. At this point, a stage director could focus some attention on Fasolt.

At point C, the violin plays Freia's motive, which generally indicates a measure of innocence, sympathy, and vulnerability. Wagner highlights the motive statement with the oboe, denoting tragedy. The cello accompaniment gains presence with the addition of viola, and eventually violin.

At point D, the large woodwind voicing suggests obstacles for Alberich. Then, it dissolves into chords of three different colors: bass clarinet-bassoon (gloom; hate), clarinet (Nibelungs), and horn (nobility). Perhaps this refers to the wide variety of beings that Loge surveyed.

The violin plays a variation of Freia's motive at point E when Loge asks, "What does man hold mightier than woman's joy and worth?" Rather than highlight woman's fairness as he did the first time Loge asked the question, Wagner emphasizes woman's tenderness and innocence. The motive then sounds in the clarinet, which tends to characterize the Nibelungs. We might interpret this as the forces of evil subsuming the innocence and vulnerability of woman. It is a hint to Loge's most important piece of news—Alberich has stolen the gold and forsworn love. Loge's rhetorical question is far less innocent than it would seem. The horn also joins on this phrase, capturing the gods' attention to the development.

At point F, an oboe joins the group to accentuate the tragedy of the announcement to come. A brief sweep in the viola implies the laughter Loge received in answer to his question. The oboe and clarinet continue with a brief variation of the Ring motive. Although this is a unique scoring of the motive, we can infer a certain nervous cheerfulness from its light tone. Loge is relating a lighthearted moment, but the Ring motive in the

---

[43] English horn statements of other motives refer to the helplessness of captivity.

background portends much more serious news. Next, we hear a statement of Freia's motive played by the English horn followed by the horn when Loge says, "In water, earth, and air." Wagner adds a bassoon and clarinet to the woodwind group. The subtext at this point with its symbols of helplessness, fairness, despair, and Nibelung aspirations to power also foreshadows Loge's impending news. This symbolism could inform Loge's gestures, or the gods' reaction. They know there is more to the story, yet Loge withholds his most important information.

Wagner focuses attention back to Loge with a viola-cello pizzicato at point G. We hear a minor variation of the Rheingold's motive played by the horn. The subtext indicates that the noble gold is now in distress. Shortly after, at point H, a chromatic viola figure reminds us of the ungainly Alberich as he sought love from each maiden. Motive statements in the viola generally symbolize denial. In this case, the Rheinmaidens deny Alberich their love. We hear the minor variation of the Greeting to the Rheingold's motive played by the English horn-horn (despair), horn (nobility), English horn-clarinet-bassoon (Nibelung rule—echoed by clarinet and bass clarinet, symbols of Nibelung hate) as Loge announces that "The Rhine's bright children clamored their plight. The Nibelung, Night-Alberich . . ." The subtext indicates the helplessness of the Rheinmaidens at the hands of Alberich. The horn may refer to either the gold, or to the gods to whom they look for help.

At point I, the flute plays the Rheinmaidens' song, accompanied by the viola, to remind us of how the maidens denied Alberich their love. Tremolo strings heighten the suspense and agitation of the moment. The horn again plays the minor version of the Rheingold's motive at point J, against the background of clarinet-bass clarinet (Nibelung hate) and tremolo strings. We hear a statement of the Ring motive played by English horn, clarinet, and bassoon, indicating world rule for the Nibelungs. At point K, the English horn and bassoon play the minor form of the Greeting to the Gold motive, representing the maidens' wails of despair. The subtext reinforces the overt musical material as well as the sung text. It is an encapsulation of the end of scene one. Wagner paints an aural picture of the Rheinmaidens telling Loge their sad tale. A stage director might reinforce the flashback by changing the lighting or showing other reminders of scene one.

When Loge mentions Wotan at point L, the horn (nobility of the gods) plays the Greeting motive, underscored by low strings representing the darkness of the situation. A bass trumpet representing the dormant gold, followed by a trumpet-violin combination indicating the shining, innocent gold, plays the Rheingold's motive as Loge mentions returning the gold to the water. The tremolo string voicing indicates the growing emotion as the narrative grows to its climax. At this point, the stage director might choose to raise the lighting to reflect the emergence of the gold as well as the growing agitation.

The woodwind voicing that plays the Greeting motive at point M reminds us that Alberich is using the gold to gain power over the world. The motive statement changes color slightly, adding a flute and tympani. These represent the contrasting elements of lightness and force. The motive finally dissolves when the clarinet drops out, ultimately signaling despair. The stage director might drop the intensity of the lighting slightly to reflect this hopelessness, and also to signal the denouement of the narrative.

In the epilogue phrase at point N, Loge absolves himself of all responsibility for solving the problem, and places it directly onto Wotan. We hear Loge's motive played first by clarinet and bassoon, indicating the Nibelungs, then by Loge's characteristic viola-cello scoring. The orchestration shows that Loge is telling Wotan to concentrate on Alberich; he, Loge, cannot solve the problem.

Wagner's scoring choices help to foreshadow the news about Alberich. Loge knows that the first part of his speech is really about stalling and avoiding responsibility for telling important information. Even before Loge mentions Alberich and the Rheinmaidens, we hear timbres that hint at tragedy, innocence, hate, and Nibelungs.

When Loge recalls the tale of Alberich's theft, we hear some of the same sonorities from scene one. We also hear the contrasting forces of clarinet-bass clarinet (Nibelung hate) and horn (nobility). Tremolo strings add to the excitement of the moment.

When combined with the text and thematic material, Wagner's scoring symbolism helps him to paint a thorough and nuanced portrait of Loge through the narrative—Loge is a smooth bait-and-switch salesman who deflects attention from his failure to secure an alternative payment. He tells vivid tales, but hesitates to reveal the high price the gods must pay.

ANALYSIS OF SCENE THREE EXCERPT

We can utilize the symbolic properties in Wagner's orchestration to highlight subtle shades of emotion that Wagner was unable to put into his words or his themes. The following shows how interpretation of orchestral symbolism can enhance a brief segment from the third scene of <u>Das Rheingold.</u> Wotan and Loge have just descended from Valhalla to Nibelheim. They see Mime crying, and they assure him that help is on its way.

iii, 154-198	Mime:	[A]Who would help me? I have for master the truest of brothers, who places me in bondage.
	Loge:	[B]But Mime, to bind you, what gave him the might?
	Mime:	[C]With wicked craft, made [D]Alberich, [E]from the Rhine's gold, a golden ring. At its [F]great spell [G]we tremble astonished. With it, he forces us all:[H] the [I]Nibelungs' downtrodden host.[J] Once, as a carefree smiths, we made [K]jewels for our wives, beautifully forged, [L]delicate Nibelung toys. We laughed joyously as we worked.

Wagner's delicate shifts in orchestral color suggest the following interpretation. This may help the singers or stage director to understand and emphasize more of Wagner's subtext in the passage.

At Point A, Mime is accompanied by bassoons playing the Brooding motive. Wagner generally uses bassoons to refer to gloom. Loge speaks at point B. He is echoed in the orchestra by the viola, cello combination that is his characteristic accompaniment. At point C, the combination of clarinet, bass clarinet, and bassoon indicates hatred[44] on the words "with

---

[44] See article on the Ring motive.

wicked craft." Mime might also emphasize his hatred when delivering this line. Pizzicato viola and cello highlight this at point D on the word "Alberich," possibly indicating some stage motion directed at Loge, or perhaps a reaction from Loge.

At point E, on the words "from Rhine's gold, a golden ring," the combination of English horn, clarinet, bassoon, and bass clarinet appears. This relates to woodwind combinations used to refer to the idea of Alberich as world ruler. At point F, the woodwind voicing changes to oboe, English horn, bassoon, and bass clarinet. This is the only time in Das Rheingold that Wagner uses this combination, but most other instances of full double-reed plus clarinet (sometimes with bass clarinet) voicings refer to the magic of the gold. The subtext indicates the gold's power to grant world rule to Alberich.

At point G, Wagner adds the tremolo viola to underline the words "we tremble, astonished." This emphasizes the Nibelungs' constant state of mental uneasiness. The sustaining cello generally denotes privacy. It may refer to the way the Nibelungs hide from Alberich. At point H, the sustaining woodwind combination expands to include with it a clarinet. This reminds us again of the gold's magic power. Since the combination reduces to clarinet and bassoon, a scoring that often associates with the Nibelungs[45], accompanied by viola-cello pizzicatos at point I, the "Nibelung vs. Loge" symbolism suggests that Mime turns toward Loge, or that the remark merits a reaction from Loge.

At point J, on the word "host," the viola and cello accompany a horn setting of the Nibelung smiths motive. The horn scoring of this motive relates with fairness and Valhalla.[46] At this juncture, Wotan might react, as he hears about how the smiths crafted jewels for their wives. Wagner adds double basses at point K, on the phrase "jewels for our wives, beautifully forged." This adds more presence to the line, and probably indicates Mime developing his recollection, perhaps now facing front. At point L, the basses disappear, as Mime once again concentrates his attention on Loge.

---

[45] The clarinet-bassoon combination enters directly on the word "Nibelungs'."
[46] See article on Nibelung smiths motive.

This type of analysis provides greater insight into the subtext of even this small scene. Wagner offers clues, through subtle changes in timbre, to the characters' thought processes and gestures beyond his sketchy verbal indications. As a result, use of orchestral symbolism to inform dramatic detail yields a richer, more nuanced reading and performance of the opera.

SCORINGS OF MOTIVIC STATEMENTS AND THEIR SYMBOLS

Here is a list of scorings that are common to at least two leitmotives in <u>Das Rheingold</u>, along with the symbolic meanings they suggest. I have inferred the meanings by analyzing commonalities in the dramatic situations that accompany the motivic statements. Even across several motives, the dramatic content that accompanies a particular scoring is remarkably consistent. I have not included unique scorings, nor those that repeat only within one motive, such as the bass trumpet scorings of the Rheingold's motive that indicate the gold's dormant state. These examples also demonstrate a reliable link between scoring and extra-musical content, but do so in a narrower context. Scorings that appear in a variety of leitmotives provide the greatest evidence for a symbolic link.

To a certain extent, we can apply these symbols to infer subtexts from non-motivic content. The references may not be as strong as scorings linked to motivic statements. Motivic statements intentionally convey symbolic meaning, so they serve as programmatic anchors for scorings.

Three types of symbolic consistencies emerge from the scoring of <u>Das Rheingold</u>:

1) <u>Free-associative</u>--The instruments used bear no sonorous resemblance to the concept they represent, but the scoring combination recurs consistently enough that a symbolic correlation forms, such as the horn-bassoon combination used to represent payment;

2) <u>Literary-archetypal</u>--The instrument associates certain cultural attributes with its symbolic property, such as the violin representing innocence and tenderness;

3) <u>Onomatopoetic</u>--An instrument sounds like what it symbolizes, such as anvils representing smiths.

TABLE X: ORCHESTRAL SYMBOLS

Instrumentation	Symbolic association	Type of symbol
Vn	Innocence, tenderness, sympathy	Literary-archetypal
Br	Loss, denial, loneliness	Free-associative
Vc	Solitude, privacy, isolation, hidden depths	Free-associative
Vn, Br	Danger, threat, warning, dare	Free-associative
Br, Vc	Coveting, craving, Loge's character	Free-associative
Vc, Cb	Hidden in darkness, deceit	Literary-archetypal
Vn, Br, Vc	Toil, suffering	Free-associative
Full strings	Anger	Free-associative
Cl	Nibelung, scorn	Free-associative
Hb	Naïveté, tragedy, Mime	Literary-archetypal
Eng. Hn	Imprisonment, helplessness	Literary-archetypal
Fag	Gloom	Free-associative
Cl, Fag	Nibelung	Free-associative
Eng. Hn, Fag	Despair, withering, relinquishing the Tarnhelm	Free-associative

Instrumentation	Symbolic association	Type of symbol
Eng. Hn, Cl, Fag	Nibelung rule	Free-associative
Hb, Eng. Hn, Cl, Hn, Fag	Obstacle for Alberich	Free-associative
Hb, Fag, Hn, (Cl)	Nibelung aspirations to power, Mime's frustration	Free-associative
(Cl), BCl, Fag	Hate	Free-associative
KlF combinations	Mocking	Literary-archetypal
Hn, Fag	Payment	Free-associative
Hn	Freia, nobility, gods of Valhalla, justice, fairness, Donner	Literary-archetypal
Pos (CBP)	Curse	Free-associative
Tbs	Agony, dragon	Literary-archetypal
Pos, Tbs	Ill will, portrait of Valhalla	Literary-archetypal
Pauk	Warm heart, Giants' presence, force	Onomatopoetic
Cym	Cold heart, malice of command	Literary-archetypal

SUMMARY

When Wagner conceived <u>Der Ring Des Nibelungen</u>, he envisioned a tightly-packed web of meaning in which each element would reinforce the others. To that end, he exercised a degree of compositional control unheard of in his era. He wrote his own libretto, used recurring leitmotives, commissioned new instruments, and even designed his own theater. We now see that his scoring choices conveyed yet another layer of meaning to the <u>Ring</u> cycle.

<u>Das Rheingold</u> serves as our introduction to Wagner's mythical, self-contained universe. It is here that Wagner teaches us to associate leitmotives with ideas and characters, beginning in a clear and deliberate fashion. As the cycle continues, he blurs the lines between motives, allowing themes to transfigure themselves as the flow of ideas free-associates. Using a similar methodical approach, Wagner carefully links his scoring choices with shades of meaning that allow us to weave together another layer of subtext that also grows and develops, and ultimately obscures throughout the cycle. If we follow that subtext, we become privy to a deeper level of understanding of the <u>Ring</u> cycle.

It is, perhaps, a disservice to the concept of symbology to ascribe specific meanings to elements that suggest extra-musical ideas. The power of any symbol lies, in part, in its very ambiguity, its ability to convey a cluster of ideas in an oblique manner. The receiver of those ideas employs a pre-conceived set of priorities and life experiences to discern the meaning(s) behind the symbol and the way it informs the work. Thus, everyone has the potential to perceive symbolic content individually. The dynamic, highly personal nature of the interaction allows symbolic interpretation to serve as the basis for some of the most interesting discussions in the arts.

In the end, one purpose of this book is to open such a discussion, not to end it. The commonalities in <u>Das Rheingold's</u> scoring as it relates to dramatic progression are so extensive as to rule out coincidence. The connection between orchestration and drama offers new potential for understanding the self-contained universe of Wagner's <u>Ring</u>. I have proposed one set of interpretations to explain Wagner's scoring choices; there are surely others that are at least as valid.

As has been the case with leitmotives, it is not as important to narrowly label a particular scoring as it is to use the scoring as a vehicle to uncover another layer of meaning from the opera. Just as leitmotives have served to aid our understanding of the <u>Ring</u>, we can expect the orchestral symbolism in Wagner's <u>Das Rheingold</u> to help us define greater compositional unity, and to craft more sensitive, nuanced performances of the work.

ABOUT THE AUTHOR

Martin S. Richter earned a B.F.A. in Music Theory from Carnegie-Mellon University, and also studied Theory at University of Chicago and Northwestern University. He has taught Music History and Theory in adjunct and Guest Lecturer positions at Carnegie-Mellon, and won the CMU Orchestration Award in 1980. Mr. Richter has worked as a piano soloist for over thirty years.

Mr. Richter has written for Teaching K-8, and has also authored Our Living Language: Word Inventions, a classroom adaptation of Valmiki's Ramayana, and A Viking Reader. He lives in Pittsburgh, PA with his wife and daughter.

To learn more about Martin S. Richter, visit **www.martinsrichter.com**.

13556052R00076

Made in the USA
Charleston, SC
17 July 2012